Why Am I Afraid to Grieve?

Books in the same series

Series Editor: Phillip Hodson

WHY AM I AFRAID TO BE ASSERTIVE?
by Patricia Mansfield

WHY AM I AFRAID TO DIVORCE?
by Jane Butterworth

WHY AM I AFRAID TO ENJOY SEX?
by Paul Brown and Chris Kell

Why Am I Afraid to Grieve?

**Ann Carpenter
and
Geoffrey Johnson**

**Series Editor
Phillip Hodson**

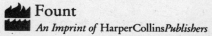
Fount
An Imprint of HarperCollins*Publishers*

Fount Paperbacks is an Imprint of
HarperCollins*Religious*
Part of HarperCollins*Publishers*
77–85 Fulham Palace Road, London, W6 8JB

First published in Great Britain
in 1994 by Fount Paperbacks

1 3 5 7 9 10 8 6 4 2

Text copyright © 1994 Ann Carpenter and
Geoffrey Johnson
Preface copyright © 1994 Phillip Hodson

Ann Carpenter and Geoffrey Johnson assert their moral
right to be identified as the authors of this work

A catalogue record for this book is
available from the British Library

ISBN 0 00 627670 9

Phototypeset by Intype, London
Printed and bound in Great Britain by
HarperCollinsManufacturing Glasgow

Contents

Preface

For many people in Britain grieving does NOT seem to come very naturally. Two world wars have changed us from Victorian 'wailers', who described in minute detail on 'grief stationery' the final agonies of the beloved, to a people who sneer at funeral processions and practise industrialized corpse-disposal. Probably the Victorians went too far but we could still learn a lot from news pictures of conflict in the Middle East, where those who feel grief in the face of death really do know how to show it. They shout! Of course, it isn't decorous, but the purpose of grief is to cope with the unacceptable, and drastic reactions are both necessary and healthy.

If you care for someone in any way, you become attached to them. If you care for someone who dies, then you continue to love them – but there is no longer a person for you to love. We cannot alter our feelings as quickly as life and death can change the world. You may begin to feel foolish about your love for a 'no one', although it is unavoidable.

The major grief feeling is LOSS. As Ann Carpenter and Geoffrey Johnson's book makes clear, we can sense this about absolutely anything that matters. We grieve in some way, often the same way, whether someone dies, or is taken from us by divorce. Or when we lose our pet cat, or move house, change schools, lose a favourite teacher or a 'best' possession. But of course the most severe loss occurs when we are bereaved by the death of someone close to us.

Naturally, the first grief feeling to hit when you get bad news is SHOCK and numbness. This is possibly nature's way of protecting us from panic and too much heartstrain.

But after a few days, or sometimes weeks, a new and far more difficult set of emotions takes over. You may feel you cannot accept that the person is dead at all (DENIAL). You may become so depressed when you do realize they are gone that you literally feel like a vegetable. Your life becomes one long ache of fatigue. This period can be quite prolonged. It is made more difficult if you can't justify the need to have these feelings at all; if you can't 'number your losses'.

Part of 'working through your grief' is to notice everything that has been taken from you, which takes time. For instance, if you've lost your father, you perhaps won't remember how Dad made the Summer Holiday successful each year until summer comes around again. Anniversaries have this effect. And so your grief will probably remain strong for twelve months at least and continue to be a problem for another twelve months after that, although don't imagine the human heart runs to a timetable. There is also a very difficult range of feelings which includes the emotion of anger, as the authors explain.

Deep inside, whatever our age, we are all like very small children. Even if someone dies tragically, we get cross because that person is DEPRIVING US of what we need. If a parent dies, the feeling is much stronger because we cannot be our own Mum and Dad. We need our parents to bring us up. So we cannot *ALLOW* them to die; it feels impossible. And again regardless of age, such feelings can get more tangled if we part on 'bad terms' with the one who has died. Then it makes us feel that our anger and hostility were almost powerful enough to *make* them die, and therefore we are dangerous and bad and very, very guilty. Or we may also realize that a bad parent is now NEVER going to love us as they should, which again feels unacceptable.

I think this book above all shows these emotions to be *normal components of grief*. If expressed, they will eventually go away. Even if you seem to be crying without end, in despair, this is actually going to bring you through at the last.

How do you know when grief has ended? The simple answer is that you are through the worst when your feeling of outraged and heartbroken loss gets replaced by a feeling of what we could call ordinary sadness. So instead of bursting into tears when the dead person is mentioned, you are able to enjoy talking about them and reminiscing despite the fact that you are conscious of the loss.

One of the most important questions is given a central place in Chapter Four – what do you say to someone who is grieving? It's almost easier to list the don'ts. For instance, never ever say, 'Try to forget it, dear, just think of the future. You'll soon get over it'. This may seem sensible at one level but the response is likely to be 'I don't want to get over it – I'm still trying to remember – I just want him back', and all you have done has made it harder for the person to remember and to grieve freely. In any case, the phrase 'getting over it' seems to imply bereavement is as trivial as a minor toothache, i.e. no big deal. 'Forget it' is in fact bad advice and in any case impossible. 'It's when you remember and it hurts that you know it really happened. That's when you begin to get better' is how another woman put it. So the best way to respond to grief in another is by trying to accept whatever they need to say or feel. 'Yes,' you say, 'I can see you feel that way about it.' And if you can spare the time to listen, encourage them to talk to you if that's their need. You don't have to give ANY advice.

In a way it's sad that this book – full of insights and real life stories – is even necessary. As a people we need convincing that strong displays of emotion will do us more good than harm. I've had a letter from a widower asking why he STILL feels upset three weeks after losing his wife! Newspapers remain full of ignorant articles sneering at counselling and grief: 'How on earth did we get through the Second World War without thousands of bereavement counsellors on hand?' (*Daily Mail*, 7 January 1994). The answer is of course 'at great cost and with lasting damage to most British families'.

Phillip Hodson

Introduction

This book is about grief arising, not just from death, but from all kinds of loss. Between us we have experienced – like most other people – a range of losses. This includes the death of a child, the break-up of parents, our own previous divorces, redundancy, many house moves, loss of faith, changes of direction, fresh starts. Out of these experiences we have come to think hard on loss and grief and what other people go through. We haven't necessarily come to terms with all our own experiences – and we certainly don't have all the answers regarding other people's – but what we have discovered is that we can all be more understanding of others who are in a grieving situation, and certainly less hard on ourselves. Grief does involve a whole series of responses including disbelief, denial, sorrow, anger, guilt and, hopefully, acceptance. If we can at least concede that all these responses are largely normal, then we will all be helped on the road to recovery.

The personal experiences featured in this book are drawn from 'real life' and all names have been changed. The experiences which are written in the first person are those of one or other of the authors.

Ann Carpenter and
Geoffrey Johnson

CHAPTER 1

What is Grief?

We can all expect to experience grief, to some degree, at some point in our lives. Grief is a response to loss – often the death of a loved one; but it can also be a response to other kinds of loss such as loss of job, home, or a sense of identity, as well as the break-up of a relationship. Grief is a normal part of life; none the less, when we experience it we often ask 'Why is this happening to me?' or 'What have I done wrong?'

The temptation is to think that we are the only ones to whom this dreadful thing has ever happened. This may be due partly to the fact that, in modern-day living, space for mourning has been squeezed out, as has time to share grief. It is no longer usual to wear black – even at a funeral – to signal death through window drapes or to enter a socially accepted period of mourning. In certain circumstances we will be given a day or two off work but, very speedily, all will be back to 'normal'. Tolerance for the bereaved is relatively short-lived. A specified period of mourning not only enables people to express their grief more freely, it also tells others what is happening – a vital and highly underrated component of the grieving experience. Death, dying, unhappiness or pent-up anger through bereavement have become taboo subjects. There is little opportunity to share experiences, become more informed and perhaps realize that other people are going through the same trauma. No wonder we can feel so isolated.

A RANGE OF CAUSES

The extent to which we experience grief will, of course, depend on many factors. A prime influence will naturally be the exact cause of our sorrow, and how we react to this will largely depend on the kind of people we are. Our own personalities, inner resources, experience of life, age, background and culture will all play a part. There may also be variations in our reactions according to whether we are men or women. Another important aspect will be outside circumstances – both connected and unconnected – which may affect us during our period of grieving.

It is generally accepted that the greatest cause of grief is the death of someone close. This can have a devastating affect on those left behind and reactions vary: they can be immediate, may come much later, can be of a relatively short length of time, or long and drawn out over a period of years. Because we are all individuals, there can be no 'blueprint' for the grieving process.

It can also have a 'knock on' effect. For example, when a spouse dies there is more than just the loss of a sexual partner and companion at stake. Finances may be greatly reduced leading to insecurity and a change of lifestyle. Then there's the added burden of society reacting differently to the partner left behind. Widows and divorced women speak of former 'friends' who suddenly stop inviting them round because they are no longer part of a couple. They relate how other women suddenly perceive them as a threat. This appears to happen to women more than to men.

WHY AM I AFRAID TO GRIEVE?

Grief may be painful but it is a normal and necessary experience. So why do most of us fear it? Grieving means feeling deeply and hurting badly. It is about sensing hopelessness, confronting helplessness, experiencing heartbreak. It may involve digging up long-buried feelings which you would rather had remained buried. Change becomes inevitable.

Change is something which many of us fear and most of us resist. Coping with change can range from a favourite store closing and having to find somewhere new to buy groceries to moving to a completely new area. It can mean the imminent arrival of a new boss or, increasingly likely these days, the entire company being sold and the prospect of redundancy looming. With change we are usually convinced the alternative won't be as good and generally fear the worst.

All in all, grief with its accompanying baggage is a difficult load to bear. It is hardly surprising that many of us would avoid the experience altogether if we could. But grief is not all bad. It is certainly an unhappy experience but it can also be constructive, helping us survive our loss. It may even bring its own rewards through better self-understanding and fresh directions which actually enhance life.

WHAT TO EXPECT

It must be stressed that there is no 'blueprint' for the grieving process. There is, however, a general pattern. Grief is a combination of emotions, a series of feelings. They do not necessarily come in the same order and, while some of us go through a whole range of responses – both emotional and physical – others only experience one or two. Here are some examples of how a diverse cross-section of people have reacted to grief:

When AUDREY learned of her husband's death in a road accident she was so shocked she didn't speak at all for several days.

Life had never been easy for Audrey. She had been born into a large family but had been pushed aside by everyone because she tended to be a slow learner. A special school and dedicated teachers had helped her along the way but happiness had only come when she married.

Sid was twenty years older and had been forced by a pit accident to give up his job. Most days, Sid and Audrey cycled off to work on their allotment. Together they gardened, fished and shopped and built up a companionable and satisfying life.

When, one Thursday afternoon, a policeman arrived on the doorstep, Audrey was surprised but not alarmed. He was young but thoughtful and had first established that a neighbour in the next-door house was at home. As gently as he could, he explained to Audrey that Sid had been killed in a road accident.

Audrey went very white. She said, 'I don't believe it - are you joking? You ought not to say such things.' But soon she showed that she understood and believed what she had been told. For several days after this she didn't speak at all. Much later she expressed her initial reactions: 'I felt as cold as ice but then I went very hot and couldn't breathe properly; I needed air. I couldn't cry and I just wanted to hit the policeman for telling me what I didn't want to know.'

TRACEY was totally unprepared for the numbness she felt at the news of her grandmother's death.

Tracey's grandmother had been an active and ever-present member of the family. One day, when Tracey returned home from work, she was completely shocked to hear of her grandmother's death. She said:

> I was horrified and just couldn't believe it. I know Grandma had always complained of various ailments but I just didn't take her seriously - which also made me feel terribly guilty later on. But at the time all I could do was cry. I just sobbed and sobbed and couldn't think rationally at all. This lasted for days. I don't remember much about anything just after that - the arrangements for the funeral, the service itself - anything. It was all a blur.

This was the first time that Tracey had personally experienced the death of someone close to her, and death was not something that was discussed in the family. It was feared, rather than seen as an inevitable part of life.

DAVID could not accept the changing circumstances of his job.

The management structure of the large institution changed and managers had to reapply for jobs they had actually been working in for some time, but which now had a different title. Applying for the seventh time for his own senior post caused David some anxiety and frustration but no great alarm since he had always been successful. However on this occasion, to his total disbelief, he was not appointed.

David's working circumstances were unique in that, unlike most of the other staff, he had actually engineered a 'no dismissal' clause into his contract. As far as he was concerned he had a job for life. The management accordingly decided to promote him 'sideways' and David ended up in a position without any influence or responsibility.

None the less, David decided to continue to go to work in the same office, to send out memos under the same title and meet with the same circle of colleagues whom he called to his office. This continued for six months. David had always been a powerful figure and, despite the new appointee making his position more or less redundant, he continued to exercise a degree of influence for a considerable period of time.

'They won't get rid of me that easily' was a typical comment. However, colleagues closest to him began to realize that other emotions were at work. They could see that David was trying to deny that anything had changed. He simply couldn't let go of all that he had worked for.

When JANET's husband had a stroke leaving him speechless and with no memory of her, Janet felt he had let her down. Her reaction was one of anger.

Her marriage to Bill when she was very young had turned out well. He had a daughter, not that much younger than Janet, by his first marriage and there had been some criticism from Janet's parents. But Bill, an active, sporty man, had been a lively, good-natured husband and a patient father to their two children.

It was an immense shock when Bill had a stroke, leaving him virtually speechless and with severe brain damage. During his long stay in hospital, Janet became increasingly distressed. She realized that Bill would never again be the same man she had once loved. To house him appropriately meant she would have to completely change her home, lifestyle and perhaps give up her job. This was too hard for Janet to accept. She decided that the only course of action was to arrange for Bill to go into a nursing home. Janet said:

> People probably think I am wicked but Bill just isn't my husband any more. He doesn't even know me, he can't talk to me or share any of the memories we had together. Understanding that he can't help himself doesn't make things any easier for me. I am angry and hurt and feel he has let me down.
>
> I can hardly bear to look at him and I don't really ever want to see him again. No one has the right to expect me to change my life when Bill could die at any time. I could sell my house and give my job up to look after him and then suddenly he could be gone – leaving me with nothing.

DOROTHY could not come to terms with her mother's death. She raged at God for letting it happen.

Since her mother's death, she had struggled for months with the tears that welled up and spilled over each time she remembered incidents from their life together.

One day when she was out shopping, she saw the new curate from her local church. Dorothy had been a faithful and regular member all her life. She approached the young man, intending to introduce herself but, to her surprise, she found herself saying:

> I have been a member of St John's for many years and my mother's funeral was held there six months ago. I didn't feel the vicar said anything very special about her, even though Mother had been a lifelong member of the congre-

gation. I honestly don't think I shall ever go to your church again. There is so much talk about a loving God, but how could he be loving when he let my mother die? I can never believe in God again nor will I ever go to church again.

The young priest was somewhat taken aback by this outburst; however, he tried his best to listen and understand the strength of this stranger's feelings. Then, seeing that the former parishioner was not young herself, he asked how old Dorothy's mother had been when she died. 'My mother was ninety-six,' came the reply. 'She spent all her life doing good for others. Why did she have to die?'

After losing his job, HARRY felt great guilt at having to rely on his wife's income and support.

He had been employed in the building trade since leaving school and had become not only a skilled craftsman but also a foreman with responsibilities. He enjoyed his work and was committed to the company that had promoted him.

Then recession hit the firm and suddenly, for Harry, there was no alternative to accepting redundancy. It was a hard blow to have to start looking for a job again at fifty-four. Harry had made lots of contacts in the building trade and soon decided to become self-employed within a co-operative. All went well to begin with but then he had to undergo a serious operation which meant taking quite a lot of time off. Soon after returning to work, Harry had an accident. His colleagues in the co-operative decided they had to replace him and Harry found, at fifty-nine, that work had dried up altogether.

He was shattered. He had prematurely lost a lifelong career; self-employment meant he couldn't claim benefits although he had paid National Insurance for forty years.

It's bad enough not working and having little hope of ever working again. What really hurts is Christmas and not being able to buy presents for the family. My wife's anniversary present was only chocolates and now it's her birthday I can afford nothing. Why should she have to suffer because I have lost my job? She still works to support us both and I just don't think it's fair on her.

Moving to a picturesque village opened old wounds for SARAH and led to depression.

Her parents' divorce left her living with her grandparents and mother. Separation from her father, her mother's remarriage and the ensuing continuous house and school moving left her a rootless and unhappy teenager with few friends. But she was both imaginative and ambitious and, after leaving home, she made a new life for herself in London. Eventually she bought her own flat and secured a good job and a circle of friends.

In her thirties she married and left London to live in a village. Many of her friends envied her opportunity to live what they perceived as an idyllic countryside lifestyle, with village amenities and surrounded by beautiful countryside. But despite her own expectations, Sarah felt unhappy while she lived there. Soon after moving to the village Sarah started to become resentful, unsettled and depressed. After five years the couple returned, not to London, but to town life. Sarah said:

> For the past five years I have been depressed without understanding why. Making a new circle of friends was certainly much harder than I expected and, to be honest, most of the local clubs and groups involved activities that we didn't enjoy. Looking back at my years in London, I realize that was the one time I felt really secure and 'at home'. I had friends, was part of a community and led a stable life – all things I didn't have as I was growing up. Living in that village was like returning to the lonely, isolated existence of those early years.

BETTY appeared to ignore her increasing ill-health but in fact she had come to accept it.

She loved her job as a domestic for a large institution and she led a full social life outside work. She and her husband had no children but had several nephews and nieces and were 'uncle' and 'aunt' to many of their friends' children, too. When, in her early fifties, she had to undergo a mastectomy, she took it in her stride.

In her late fifties, problems arose once more, sometimes keeping her off work. Again she stood up to the illness and did all that the medical staff suggested including exercising regularly, revising her diet and taking care to rest. When she did manage to work, she looked increasingly ill but made it clear to her colleagues that she had no wish to talk about ill-health.

Her friends and staff at the physiotherapy clinic became concerned that Betty was denying her illness and its seriousness. One day her hospital consultant needed to interview her. Betty explained:

> He carefully closed his office door so I knew he had some serious talking to do. He started by saying, 'There is something you must know', but of course he didn't have to tell me anything. I asked him how long I had to live and if I would see my wedding anniversary in six months' time. He replied, 'That's hard to say.' All right then, shall I reach my sixtieth birthday? Again he seemed uncertain. I finally put it to him that he was telling me I'd better make any plans I needed to make pretty quickly. 'Yes', he replied, 'you have weeks rather than months to live; we can never say exactly.'

Betty treated herself to a taxi home and, over the next few days, made sure all outstanding bills were paid and that her husband's finances were in order. She sorted out jewellery, personal items and arranged Christmas presents. Within weeks she died painlessly – and peacefully.

UNDERSTANDING OUR RESPONSES

Each of these personal experiences illustrates a different aspect of what has come to be recognized as a natural process. When we are in a grief situation we are often taken aback by these feelings. Perhaps they are foreign to us and we feel we are acting out of character. We may view them with some alarm – as though we are being taken over and will never quite be our old selves again.

Grief responses have a life of their own; however rational we try to be, we often simply have to succumb to bouts of depression, anger or weeping. There is a fine line between the need for self-discipline and the need also to let out our emotions: keeping our emotions 'under control' in times of great stress can harm us physically as well as emotionally. Suppressed emotions also have a habit of bobbing back up later on in life.

One man described his experience this way: 'I felt as though the world was going on outside but had nothing to do with me. It was as though I was frozen in time.' Other people have described a sensation of standing aside and looking down on themselves as they go through a series of emotions. One woman likened it to the washing machine set in action with no control over the buttons. 'The exaggerated action of clothes being soaked, washed, rinsed, spun then tumble dried could be compared to how I was feeling at the time – totally "washed out".' She could peer in through the glass door and take note of the precise spot which the process had reached, but there was no speeding it up or even resetting the buttons for a different programme.

The grieving process may include some or all of the following recognizable stages but to fix it to a predictable schedule or time scale is inadvisable.

Shock/Disbelief

When unexpected news arrives there are shock waves of reaction. At first we may fail to comprehend the words we are hearing. It's as though the mind is resisting receiving the information. This can also happen, incidentally, when the news we are being given is not totally unwelcome. It could, for example, be about a surprise promotion or an unexpectedly successful examination result.

When the news is bad, reactions can be physical as well as mental. They can range from collapse, fainting and loss of physical strength to becoming as white as a sheet, welling up of tears and uncontrollable weeping.

Audrey felt first frozen then boiling hot. She kept pulling at the neck of her sweater because she could not breathe properly and felt she needed air. It also left her speechless. Those first reactions, initiated by the sudden and totally unexpected news, had begun a life cycle of their own. Audrey's good health and future happiness would depend on their appropriate resolution.

Both Tracey and Audrey had family and friends to provide support and act as an additional source of strength. But in a fragmented society there is often no shoulder to cry on through the bereavement stages. Fortunately, this situation has given rise to the support-group movement which provides greatly needed comfort for those who would otherwise find themselves isolated. Initially offering general support these groups have now evolved to provide specific support for precise needs and widely differing experiences of loss.

Denial

Although we all react to situations in individual ways, we also have a natural reflex response. If someone takes a swing at us, we duck – or take a swing back. The DIY enthusiast will be well aware of the natural verbal response to a hammerblow which hits fingers instead of the nail!

To defend ourselves against the hurt of unacceptable news, the mind either fails to comprehend or tries to accept preferred, alternative information. Although it had crossed David's mind that he might not be reappointed to his senior management position, in the event, he resisted the reality of the situation. When a junior colleague was awarded the post, and David was 'moved sideways', he managed to deny this decision. His office remained in the same place (the new appointee was actually given a smaller and less conveniently placed office) and, out of loyalty, staff continued to deal with him as though nothing had changed. At first they admired his fight against what they perceived as the stupidity of those in authority but, as the situation continued, it became clear that David was becoming increasingly morose and demoralized by his loss of status and removal from a recognized network of influence.

David had been a lifelong nurse dedicated to the care of

vulnerable people, working in an institution that was supposed to offer a healing environment. Now he had become the vulnerable one and he felt he was being badly and unfairly treated. Both to protect himself and to protect the worth of his work within a 'caring institution' he had to deny what had happened to him.

Anger

Anger has had a bad press. Among the seven deadly sins, anger comes second to pride, followed closely by lust. Anger has historically been rejected by white, Anglo-Saxon Protestant communities. They consider it bad and wrong. No wonder that anger often seems the most difficult of emotions to handle and with which to come to terms.

In grief, anger flares up. Sometimes it is directed fittingly and, at other times, can seem totally inappropriate. Observers can be led to make judgements about those who were angry – or avoid them altogether.

Dorothy was angry with both the church and God after her mother died. To her own surprise, this anger manifested itself when she met the young curate in the street. She probably hadn't meant to lose her temper but circumstances suddenly provided the opportunity. Naturally the curate was taken aback; none the less he accepted the situation and remained calm at Dorothy's sudden outburst of emotion. Because he allowed Dorothy to express her feelings, it is possible that he enabled her to move on emotionally.

Dorothy's church community, however, could not cope with an elderly woman's anger, nor could it provide the support that she so badly needed. Dorothy never did return to church. She obviously needed additional help in order to successfully navigate her private sea of suffering. Revising her opinion of church and God might have proved of lasting benefit to Dorothy but her fellows in the church community were frightened off by her rage. Despite her many years of church attendance there wasn't enough community support to draw her back in. To lose mother, God and a lifelong community of friendship in her church must have resulted in great loneliness.

This case illustrates, in addition, society's attitude to anger in the elderly. We have this idea that old people are benign and sweet-natured and that somehow our capacity for passionate feelings will evaporate into thin air as we move into old age.

In Janet's case, the sudden illness of her husband Bill brought many other problems. Through no fault of either partner, a relatively young wife had been left with a terrible burden. Her husband was now severely limited, totally dependent and no longer the companion, lover and support he had once been. 'I feel angry and hurt and feel he has let me down,' she said. 'I can hardly bear to look at him and I don't really ever want to see him again.' The fact that Bill had exercised regularly and ate healthily, that he had neither been a drinker nor a smoker, and had taken care to try to keep youthful made no difference. That there could be no blame attached to his circumstances was irrelevant. Janet's ensuing feelings of rage were genuine and could not fail to be expressed – as in Dorothy's case. In many other situations where different personalities and circumstances are involved, anger is all too often bottled up and locked away from view.

Janet did, eventually, start divorce proceedings and made plans for the proper care of her husband. Many would consider her actions selfish and perhaps even wicked but the fact she was able to express her outrage at both her husband, his illness and the affect this had on her own life played an important part in helping her rebuild it. After initially feeling unable to see Bill, this also enabled her to start and continue to visit him regularly in his nursing home.

Guilt and Depression

Closely associated to anger are guilt and depression, both of which can be extremely disabling. It would seem that Sarah had everything for which to be grateful. She had a larger and more attractive home than she could have afforded had she remained living in London. Surroundings were peaceful, green and unspoiled. There was never any question about the pleasure she gained from her new – and first ever – garden. Even being made redundant during the period of her stay in the village was quickly followed by the chance of a part-time job which, if not particularly satisfying, was convenient. Yet the ongoing sense of gloom and pessimism clung to her like a limpet. However many times she checked the list of positive things in her life the weight of heaviness continued to infect her outlook and her relationships.

Harry's sense of helplessness was very real, as was his anxiety about the future. But the pervading and inescapable pressure that gnawed away at him, and which he didn't seem to be able to stop talking about, was his sense of guilt. Although he had been a devoted husband and had brought up two sons who now appeared settled in their adult lives, Harry still felt that he had failed his wife. Rather than being able to provide her with the prospect of a secure and comfortable retirement, after only six months of unemployment he was having to dig into their savings just to pay the usual household expenses. Harry had never been terribly imaginative in his present-giving and had often fallen back on a gift of money. Since this was now impossible, a paltry box of chocolates only underlined, in his mind, the extent of his hopelessness.

It was clear from how his wife had responded to their difficulties, and what she had actually told him, that she loved him and wanted to ease his overwhelming sense of responsibility for her life. To improve things financially, she was able to increase the hours of her part-time job. She reassured Harry that their present difficulties were not a reason for blaming himself and reminded him that friends and neighbours were facing the same kinds of problems. But however much she tried to allay his fears, he still felt inadequate that she had to work harder to support them both. 'Why should she have to suffer because I have lost my job?' he asked. This illustrates just how effectively the power of feelings can smother reason in times of grief.

For Harry, the sense of guilt continues. Sarah, however, has left her depression behind with the village. Some of the childhood feelings that overwhelmed and haunted her had been comprehended and exorcised during that period of time. In order to see them in perspective and throw off the burden of gloom, she also needed to move to totally different surroundings.

Depression and guilt often have much in common. Both contain elements of helplessness and hopelessness. Both are feelings that are turned inwards and are directed at the sufferer rather than others. They are repressed rather than expressed passion.

Acceptance

It is always a mistake to jump to conclusions, to try to predict how others will react – or make judgements about the way they do react. There is also the temptation to view a situation from our own standpoint, applying our own characteristics and experiences. This can not only prove extremely unhelpful, it can also add to the burden that others carry. Individuals are usually very surprising in the way they react to loss and crisis.

To her close friends and colleagues, Betty gave every appearance of ignoring or denying the seriousness of her illness. At the clinic, where the physiotherapists grew to admire her buoyant courage, they regularly discussed whether or not to broach the subject of her developing illness. But whenever they made an attempt to explore the implications of her increasing limitations, Betty just laughed and insisted, 'If my right arm won't work I always have got the left one!' She would not be deterred from confronting the challenges of living. 'Nothing is going to beat me, if I can help it,' was her constant refrain.

Betty's spirit of optimism persisted for weeks into months and eventually continued over a period of three or four years. She never allowed having to use crutches to deter her from going on holidays abroad and was always well prepared for any relapses in her health – although she did have to return home earlier than intended several times. Eventually, even the therapists were persuaded by Betty's confidence and enthusiasm. So, instead of enduring several years of emotional turmoil, despite physical inconvenience and a fair amount of pain, she maintained her enjoyment of life.

For Betty it was important to try to carry on as normally as was possible. But, when the end of her life did finally arrive, she was totally prepared. Recalling her interview with the hospital consultant Betty said; 'He started by saying, "There is something you must know" but of course he didn't have to tell me anything.' When Betty finally understood the inescapable necessity of facing the approaching conclusion of her life, she wanted to know the facts.

She actually wanted to spare the consultant the necessity of having to be completely blunt. She said that she had no fears of death herself but she thought it must be terribly hard for a medical man, who had worked so hard to keep her going, to then have to admit that there was no more that he could do for her.

Through the consultant's hesitation Betty quickly deduced that she would be unlikely to celebrate her next wedding anniversary or her birthday. She then realized that the plans she would have to make must be carried out pretty speedily. Within the week she had everything in hand. As she wanted to die in her own home, special nursing had to be organized. Her husband's needs were discussed, and financial matters sorted out. Over the next few days friends, relatives and colleagues from work were given the opportunity to spend a little time with her.

Although now quite obviously much weaker, Betty had gained much peace of mind that all that needed to be attended to was completed. Her last two days were very quiet, with just two visits from nurses and the company of her husband and two close friends. She died peacefully and painlessly leaving behind a sense of sorrow, admiration and great gratitude.

PERSONAL RESOURCES

Of all the people described here, Audrey apparently had the least available personal resources on which to draw. On the face of it, she had limited intellectual abilities, few apparent prospects of work or alternative options of lifestyle. She had extremely good-hearted and kind neighbours but her family background provided little warmth or stability.

However, despite these and other drawbacks, and against all the odds, Audrey met and married another man within a year of her first husband's death. She had the inner resources to gradually confront the pain of her emotions and drag herself back into the land of the living.

It would have appeared to his colleagues that David was totally mentally ill-equipped to make a new life for himself after all those years in the same management job, and from his apparent resistance to the reality of his change of circumstances. But although he could not actually have been made redundant from his management post, after six months he elected to take early retirement.

Since he had a natural aptitude for languages, he gained a university place and began a completely new phase in his life. David was able to admit that, in his youth, he had always regretted not going to university and that perhaps there was now the possibility to fulfil an almost forgotten dream.

Pain of any sort – physical, emotional or spiritual – drives the individual into him or herself. They may appear self-absorbed, self-centred or downright selfish to the unsympathetic and uninformed observer but, they, and we, are trying to do the best we possibly can with the inner resources at our disposal.

It is easy to say Dorothy was foolish to blame God for letting her very elderly mother die. Most of us would count ourselves extremely fortunate to live to such an age, providing we had enjoyed good health up to the end, as Dorothy's mother had done.

Was it not time for Harry to recognize how lucky he was to have such an able and understanding wife? Perhaps he needed to appreciate that she was not only able to take good care of herself, but could well take responsibility for them both.

It would not have been difficult to find dozens of people only too ready and willing to swap the chaos and dirt of the London suburbs for the rural life that Sarah had moved to. Her country dwelling and peaceful environment were to be envied. Shouldn't she just get a grip on herself and snap out of her pessimistic depression?

Perhaps the most difficult of all to understand was the apparent heartlessness of Janet. Surely many other wives would have buckled down to the responsibilities forced upon them by a partner's illness. Had she really been an unfeeling and selfish woman, she would not have experienced such desperate rage. Undoubtedly the outward expression of these feelings, directed at her husband and at those she knew disapproved of her behaviour, resulted from her own self-criticism. Indeed, she directed many of the same accusations at herself. With this in mind, it probably took a great deal of strength for Janet to arrive at her final decision.

Bill continued in his incapacitated state for some time but, because of the decisions Janet had taken, she was able to make his life in the nursing home as comfortable as was possible. Eventually, she did make another relationship and together with her new partner continued to visit Bill regularly – although he neither knew nor could recognize her.

Here is a short exercise to try that will help you reflect on your own losses:

Take a sheet of paper and a pen and draw a straight line across the paper from left to right. On the left-hand end of the line write 'Birth' and on the right 'Today'. Now, using the line as the time scale between your birth and where you are now, mark on it the losses that you have experienced in your life. Try to remember them all – they could include incidents such as moving schools and losing friends, losing a pet or later, a job.

The object of this exercise is to give yourself a chance to quietly reflect on your own life and to work out:

- What losses you have experienced;
- When those losses took place in your life;
- How you feel about those losses now.

CHAPTER 2

What is the Source?

Death may be a root source of grief but many other types of loss cause us to mourn. In the previous chapter we established four major points:

- It is normal for the experience of loss to arouse a response of grief.
- There is a recognizable grieving process.
- Individuals respond in a unique manner. While there are definite stages in the process, a blueprint cannot be applied in a mechanical way.
- Evidence of the effects of grieving are seen in every aspect of the individual's life – in body, mind and spirit.

All the personal experiences in chapter 1 could have been composed of situations where death was the significant cause of the loss experienced. Betty's story was an example of terminal illness that led to a very personal response to the approach of death. Bereavement, through the death of a loved family member, was experienced by Audrey, Tracey and Dorothy. But alongside these were other losses – of employment, or a husband and companion through illness, and loss of a lifestyle through moving house.

Job loss and all its implications are becoming increasingly relevant these days. As well as having to cope with the stress of financial pressures and lack of self-esteem, losing a job can also mean being moved from one post to another or being demoted, and perhaps having to deal with a different working role, a new boss, less responsibility, reduced credibility or a lower salary.

Moving from one location to another is well recognized as a source of great stress – for a variety of different reasons. Loss of a well-known neighbourhood and a reliable network of friends is looked upon by some as a great opportunity, by others as a challenge, but by very many of us as a great, and often unwelcome, upheaval. In our illustration, however, a house move also aroused emotions related to an earlier period of Sarah's life, in which she had not been happy.

PIONEERING WORK

There's a wealth of knowledge and insight behind our comprehension of how the grieving process works and exactly how powerful – and necessary – it is. This has sprung largely from pioneering work in the field of care for the terminally ill.

The explorations, struggles and courage of both carers and those they have cared for has led to this knowledge. Many dying people have been prepared to dig through the pain of their own experiences in the belief that it might be possible to help others who tread the same path.

The courage of the carers has also played a vital part and deserves recognition. Until quite recently the accepted and unchallenged wisdom was that the dying patient must not be told of his or her condition – under any circumstances. It was firmly believed that, in the majority of cases, the human spirit was unable to cope with the reality of mortality. In addition to this, most medical practitioners were firmly of the opinion that to 'burden' the patient with such bad news was neither therapeutic nor would it prove of any value to them as they died. Some medical professionals, however, were not happy with this arrangement. Those who could no longer comply with, what they perceived as, the dishonesty of hiding the truth from their patients, risked a great deal of personal criticism and professional censure by going against this well-intentioned but ultimately destructive view.

Over the past twenty years, research has proved beyond the shadow of a doubt that where openness and careful response to people's wishes are exercised, the quality of life in those last days, weeks or even months can be preserved and protected. In fact, to hide the truth from the terminally ill can actually cause additional upset. Today, largely as a result of the dedicated style of care shown by the hospice movement, much additional heartache is avoided through greater attention being given to the feelings and wishes of the dying patient.

Not everyone finds it acceptable to learn of the nearness of their death. But in the majority of cases it would appear that people prefer honesty.

The human spirit, far from being diminished by the confrontation with individual mortality, appears to respond – and grow. The chance to know the truth and to 'grieve' may well lift someone from the brink of helplessness. It can provide them with the opportunity to come to terms with their past. They are then able to move forward positively to the business of 'dying well'. The effects of sharing 'bad news' can be seen to be 'enabling' rather than 'disabling'.

WIDER ASPECTS OF LOSS

It quickly became clear that exactly the same grieving process was at work in people other than those facing their own death. The same process was to be seen in the 'bereaved' – those who were left behind. Whether the loss was that of a parent or a child, a close friend or a working colleague, the loss of a loved one could be seen to trigger the same dynamic processes.

Facing the reality of both personal dying and bereavement went on to provide a springboard for active attention to all aspects of loss. Death was placed alongside the other kinds of bereavement that we were likely to experience in the normal life cycle. Now there is a deeper understanding of the grieving required after the breakdown of family relationships, enforced separations – even the loss of a valued understanding of life be it religious, political or moral. In our own varied ways we grieve for loss of youth, looks or sexual powers.

It can even stem from national or world problems as well as personal traumas. Communities grieve, as do nations. Tragedies such as Hillsborough and the murder of small children are marked by mountains of wreaths and flowers, community memorial services and outbursts of communal rage.

None of us can be protected from loss. Adults try to avoid bad news by switching off the television and quickly turning over the pages of the newspaper. Parents endeavour to protect their children from shocks, trials and hardships. But, to try to hide from trauma is both dangerous and self-defeating. There is ample evidence to suggest that the young as well the more mature will experience grief after loss. Given proper support, young children will cope as well as the more mature person. There is much we can all do to prepare ourselves for loss by looking at life more openly and realistically.

This next group of personal histories illustrates loss in a few of its many different forms. It also observes a wider variety of individual and group responses.

For DENISE and MARTIN, both in their fifties, early retirement meant the realization of a long-held dream. But unexpected events overtook their carefully laid plans.

They had always loved the English countryside so, when their two children were independent, they carefully planned for Martin's early retirement. After gaining all the necessary professional business advice they bought a shop in a small West Country town. It soon became clear that they had chosen astutely. It was well worth working hard since the shop was a success, the couple were popular and they enjoyed every minute of their new life.

One icy morning, meeting the delivery van in the small car park beside the shop, Denise had a fall. It shook her up a bit but didn't seem to cause any other obvious problems. In the succeeding weeks, however, other symptoms developed and, soon after, multiple sclerosis was diagnosed. Denise was admitted to the general hospital in the nearest town, fifteen miles away. Over the next few months there were not only regular visits to the hospital but also lengthy stays.

The success of the shop had been the result of the pair working as a team, each contributing their individual abilities. Martin was a natural communicator. He was cheerful and friendly and had a genuine desire to see that his customers got what they required. Denise turned out to be the business woman and the one who converted customer needs into a recipe for business success. But now the partnership had been broken and, since all their savings had been ploughed into the business, their livelihood was at stake as well as Denise's health.

Obviously Denise was no longer well enough to contribute her administration skills and, naturally enough, Martin started to lose his good-natured approach to his work. If their longed-for and once-thriving business was not to decline any more, they would have to rethink how the store was run and pay for assistance – not least to cover for Martin when he needed to be at the hospital with Denise.

An active retirement does not mean that life gets any easier. GRACE, in her early seventies, tried to make 'getting older' have some meaning.

She had always tackled working life with great gusto and when retirement was finally forced upon her she virtually laid siege to her new lifestyle. She had managed to continue her job until well after her sixty-fifth birthday and, even into her seventies she was called upon to provide cover at holiday times or in the event of staff shortage.

The University of the Third Age provided stimulation for her to develop language skills, as well as guiding her in how to get articles published. She was also hard at work writing a novel. Grace was determined to utilize her varied experiences of growing up in a Jewish area of London in the 1920s and 30s, her exploits in the Forces during the war, and the richness of her working life. There was so much that she still wanted to achieve, but life remained basically unsatisfactory for her.

Grace's health was relatively good and her memory and thoughts were as clear as a bell. As with most people, she had worries that plagued her at times: anxiety about her son, who had a young family and had recently been made redundant; a daughter, too far away in a foreign country, although she had managed a couple of visits. However, her greatest source of concern was her husband, who was several years her senior. She said:

> Like everyone in our generation we have had to fight but, when we were younger, we fought together. Now in old age we have so little in common. I never found him a wildly exciting man, but he was a faithful husband and he was good with the children. I miss the physical side to our lives, but what is harder to bear now is the lack of any other affection. He never puts his arm round me, buys me a present or flowers. There is no feeling of affection for me whatsoever.

In retirement, Grace had tried to make a new life for herself, but it seemed that whatever she tried to do, she was constantly rebuffed by those around her. Even a long-awaited visit from the daughter who lived abroad ended in tears and resentment. Grace was a disappointed woman with a great capacity to upset those with whom she came in contact.

JOHN had always considered himself to be a physical man yet marriage caused him to lose his self-respect and sexual identity.

Although he hadn't come from a religious family, like so many other children he had been packed off to Sunday School each week. Soon, the Christian faith developed into a powerful influence in his life.

He had always been a very physical man who was active in many sports. He was also well aware that sex was very important to him. But when he married, although the physical side of the relationship was vital to him, he also wanted a partner who could share his work and ideals. John and his wife did not have sexual intercourse until after they were married and, from the honeymoon onwards, they ran into sexual difficulties.

Although his wife seemed to admire and love John, she did not appear to find him all that physically attractive. For her, sex was a part of marriage which contributed to having children and, as they had decided to wait for a couple of years before starting a family, sex was rationed. The years of their marriage were to be interspersed with irregular and unsatisfactory sex and John felt very rejected, As a result of this he increasingly struggled with impotence.

When pregnancy was the goal, their sex life was mutually satisfying and very regular. Each time a child arrived John hoped that sexual activity would become an accepted part of their shared life. But on each of the three occasions he was to be disappointed and left feeling hurt and angry. His impotence became an increasing source of personal trauma and affected his confidence both in his work and in himself.

His work involved caring for people. A colleague, seeing his unhappiness and the effect it had on him, showed concern and offered physical comfort. John immediately responded to the affection, clearly understanding the implications of such a relationship. His need to feel a sexually active man was vital to his self-respect and confidence. The result of his affair was the end to his marriage, but it came as an enormous relief, rather than a loss.

His commitment to his beliefs had been undermined, not because he felt guilty, but more because he felt so angry and cheated. His wife had refused to seek help with him and, when he had tried to get help for himself, his church could offer no insight or support. John was simply asked whether he was praying about his difficulties. He replied that he couldn't pray and hadn't for months. 'Then go away and only come back when you can say the Lord's Prayer and mean it' was the only advice offered.

LYNDA's disappointment at failing to get the best job of her career turned out to be the biggest disappointment of her life.

Lynda, in her forties, had worked hard for twenty-five years. Now she was suddenly within sight of the biggest career opportunity of her life. She'd been working in a good position as deputy department head for two years when her boss fell seriously ill. Suddenly she was given the big responsibility of acting as department head during his illness. This meant much longer hours and frequent weekend work, but it was suggested to her that she may be appointed to the post if her boss was unable to return to his old job.

Lynda toiled diligently and relentlessly for several months and felt she had done the job well. However, she also nursed a feeling of slight insecurity as the managing director of the company had never actually spoken to her personally nor offered any gesture of thanks. When Lynda's boss eventually did die, as expected, she waited to see if she would be promoted. A day or two later she received a telephone call informing her that another person had been appointed to the position. She said:

I felt winded. After I put the phone down one tear trickled down my cheek, but I didn't cry. I just sat staring out of the window for most of that afternoon. It was probably the best job I would ever have a chance of getting – the best money, prestige and a real opportunity to achieve other things. I also felt it might be my last chance to do something as good.

The worst part was that I was convinced I was better at the job than the person they actually appointed – and I had a very good relationship with the rest of the staff. Although, in my heart, I wasn't greatly confident about having the good fortune to be appointed, I really thought that, given the chance, I would make a success of it. I felt I deserved it.

My husband was very supportive and anger didn't set in at first. I just felt dead and didn't want to talk about it with anyone – family, friends or colleagues. I put on an act and, looking back, I think that if I had shown I was really upset – brought it out into the open – I wouldn't have been so angry for so long. Soon after I attended an office party – although I'd rather not have gone – and I put on the best acting performance of my life. I had to greet colleagues, smile, talk to them and pretend I wasn't mortally wounded. I can honestly say that I was more upset about this than I was when my father died – probably because this grief was fuelled with anger and feelings of personal failure and therefore more complex.

I became consumed with hate and bitterness. I would like to have killed the new appointee – and the MD. I felt wounded, rejected, let down and my confidence was destroyed. No matter how much I tried to be rational about the situation I felt it must be a failing in me. If only I had got on better with the MD – been pushy, put myself about more – I might have got the job.

Eventually Lynda felt she had come to terms with the situation – although she admits she still harbours ill-will. 'It's filed away in the "grudge" file,' she smiles wryly. 'It was a missed opportunity and I am still mad with myself.'

I think the turning point came several months later when I attended a seminar with my new boss and we had the chance to talk socially – I would say we get on quite well, by the way. I suddenly realized that she was intimidated by me. I was very surprised but all at once I felt in control of the situation. For me, this was the beginning of the healing process.

ANNETTE and ROBERT prepared for loss by arranging a happy occasion.

At the agreed time, Annette and Robert arrived at the church. Their appointment was simply to arrange their wedding day and book it in the church diary. All Saints was a popular church and weddings usually needed to be booked well ahead. Although neither had ever been churchgoers, they were eager to marry quickly – in ten weeks. During the meeting, with no sense of self-pity or even sadness, they explained the reason for their haste. Annette began to talk:

Two years ago Robert started to get terribly tired playing football; he was losing energy for work, too. We have known each other since junior school and he has never been one to sit down for long. At first the doctors could not find anything wrong, but eventually diagnosed leukemia. We know now that he has not long to live. Because of that and to fit in with his treatment times we'd like to marry in ten weeks' time.

Annettte and Robert explained that this would also allow them a number of months – perhaps even a year – to enjoy a marriage relationship. Quite naturally, the vicar made every effort to work with them and their families, and the wedding day was a memorable and happy occasion.

Less than a year later, the church was even more packed than it had been for the wedding ceremony. But this time it was for Robert's funeral. It was an immensely sad occasion but the sense of admiration felt for both Annette and Robert lifted it out of the realms of tragedy. Because the loss had been both expected and shared by the couple, their family and friends, it was approached with courage which strengthened, rather than undermined, hope for the future.

ALEX, a grandmother in her sixties attached to a loved and respected partner, experienced loss of faith.

There was no blinding light in reverse; no memorable event. It was a steady leaking away from the reservoir of the commitment and way of life into which she had been born and brought up. An initial trickle of disillusionment gradually gave way to a torrent of anger and frustration.

Alex had followed a very traditional path of education and eventually went on to teach in a Roman Catholic comprehensive school. Her husband had enjoyed much the same religious upbringing but returned from two years in National Service having abandoned Church and faith. This proved no barrier to their relationship or to the education of their children in a Catholic school.

The issue of faith was never discussed in theological terms but Alex was left in no doubt that Church teaching on birth control was unacceptable to her husband. There should be no more than two children. This was no hardship for Alex as she valued her career. It did, however, make her look closely at the whole issue of birth control in the context of world population. Very gradually she considered other aspects of Church and faith, finding many inconsistencies that disturbed her. The final straw came when Alex's daughter received what she considered to be unacceptable treatment when she chose to have an abortion.

With immense sadness, Alex gave up her last regular link with all that she had learned to respect and value. Her visits to confession proved the most difficult part of her religion with which to sever ties. Looking back some years later, almost without thinking, Alex wondered aloud:

> Perhaps if I had been able to talk to my husband about the distress and disillusionment I was going through, I might have been able to weather the storm. I don't think I have had a moment's peace since I stopped going to confession. I wish I still believed but I don't, and I just cannot pretend.

Ritchie was the much-loved third member of ANDY and CLAIRE's family.

He was what is commonly called a character. He was acquired soon after Andy and Claire moved from London to the country. The couple had given up their full-time jobs, swapped a flat for a cottage that needed renovating and embarked on a drastically different style of life. Ritchie, a barrel-chested cross-breed terrier, became the third member of the family for eleven years. Claire said, 'Ritchie was all part of our new way of life; he went through everything with us.'

Andy and Claire actually moved several times and Ritchie's needs were very much part of the planning. He rewarded their careful consideration by 'taking off' at the merest sniff of a chance and returning at his leisure to present them with bits of rabbit or worse. Ritchie had great individuality and independence of spirit. One of his distinctive 'quirks' was to greet visitors on their arrival with an enthusiastic show of affection and tail wagging, then bark fiercely, furiously and somewhat disconcertingly at them as they began to leave. As well as being a faithful and dependable companion, Ritchie was also an excellent guard dog for Claire, who often worked alone in the couple's remote home. Ritchie was the first member of an extended family. He was joined by a succession of cats, an abandoned guinea fowl and, much later, by a second, more placid dog.

He became ill in the last few years of his life, making regular visits to the vet. His sight was also failing and one morning he had a bad fall down the stairs. 'He could barely stand,' said Claire. 'The vet said he'd had a mild heart attack but gave him something to help him recover. A horrendous week followed, with us each day postponing the idea of having him put down. It was a week of real soul-searching. We kept saying that we'd "see what he was like tomorrow . . ." ' Eventually, Andy and Claire made the decision to have him put down.

On returning home from the vet Andy, very much out of character, found it impossible to hide his feelings. He told Claire, 'This has been the saddest day of my life.' Claire said, 'We just put our arms around each other and cried. Unfortunately, the very next day I had to leave for a week-long Open University residential course, leaving Andy on his own.' But Andy worked through some of his sadness in a unique way.

After Claire had left for her course, Andy spent the best part of the following day building a coffin for his pet. He dug a large hole in the garden, wrapped Ritchie in his old blanket, placed his collar in the coffin and buried it. Claire described the whole thing as 'ceremonial'.

Andy and Claire felt the loss of their dog for some months afterwards. He was so much part of their lives that it seemed very strange not having him around. Claire said, 'He was part of our family and part of our history – much more so than the average dog. Our other two dogs are totally different characters; they blend into the background far more.'

The staff of SALTWOOD HOSPITAL experienced the full impact of closure on their working community.

For as long as it was possible the staff of a large psychiatric hospital put off preparing to close. Eight years became five, which then crept down to three. Then, in a ferment of activity, all the stops were pulled out and the necessary plans set in motion to transfer almost 500 patients to alternative accommodation.

The dedication and careful thought given to easing the trauma for the patients was admirable. Around 300 men and women were to be moved to another institution and, wherever possible, they were to be taken on visits to their new home and introduced to the environment and town area. Over a period of two years the transfer was achieved with much real success. Naturally, patients who had been part of one institution for great chunks of their lives grieved; but on the whole they resettled with varying depths of sadness. While such a move was far from ideal, it was a positive event for many patients because of the commitment of the staff.

What had hardly been considered was the effect on the staff of such a move. Many of them had been employed in the institution most of their working lives. In some cases, families of domestic staff and porters had worked in that same hospital over generations. Particular staff, especially night staff, had been on the same ward for twenty or more years. The psychiatric hospital was as much a community for them as for the patients. And now it was being swiftly broken up. Their working environment was going for ever.

In the early days of planning it was expected that as many as 70 per cent of the staff would be transferred to the new hospital. No more than 50 per cent accepted the option of a comparable post. Of those that did transfer, 50 per cent left within twelve months. Their denial, anger and general depression was, to a large extent, mirrored by the staff and patients at the receiving hospital. No one had given any thought to the effect of an invasion of several hundred people into their home territory.

LOCATING THE LOSS

In chapter 1, we introduced you to a range of 'everyday' people who had all struggled with grief. This could have made extremely gloomy reading if they had remained stuck in their own particular stage of grief – in anger, shock or depression – and never moved on.

There is no denying that people do become 'stuck'. It is a common feature of mourning. However, just as there is no blue-print for each individual response, there is no time-scale for when and how we move on. Some people will take days, weeks or months to resolve their sense of loss, and then there is a time when clinical intervention may be needed.

In the series of experiences we have looked at in this chapter, the focus of attention is slightly different. Rather than highlighting one particular stage of grief, we have seen sources of grief.

We can view them from a wider perspective, keeping the whole person without our sights. And the 'whole' person is comprised of three elements: the body, the mind and the spirit.

The Body

Whatever our cultural or religious view about the existence of the 'inner person', there can be no debate about the shelf-life of that outer 'packaging' – our body. In some cases the gift arrives at birth already damaged and in need of repair. In others, it can fall into disrepair through neglect or become damaged by accident. In every case the frame will need regular maintenance and the occasional overhaul. Through the senses it can be a channel of wonder, excitement and pleasure. But even when cared for responsibly it can still suddenly fail us, causing tremendous distress, upheaval – and far-reaching effects.

Denise's illness came as a complete shock. During her fifty odd years her body had undergone various usual stages, such as bearing children, and she had experienced minor ailments. However, early retirement had brought a new lease of life and fulfilment in a place she and her husband loved. The attack on her body caused more than physical pain; she had to battle with the rapidly developing bodily limitations. Confined to a wheelchair, Denise was unable to raise her arms to brush her hair or to wash properly. Regular admissions to hospital; losing much of her independence; finding even the simplest action of holding, lifting and control well beyond what she could achieve meant it was natural that she should grieve for a lost life.

Loss of bodily function, on which we depend for our contact with the world and from which we derive so much self-respect, is a bitter blow. In Denise's experience it was an all-encompassing bodily illness. For others, it could entail the loss of just one part of the frame such as a breast, a limb or even an organ. For women, in particular, the loss of looks has great consequence; for a man, the loss of physical fitness or actual bodily injury leading to the end of his ability to take part in a loved sport can have a great impact.

For Denise's husband Martin, the loss had different meaning. From one point of view his loss was also physical; the sexual partner he had loved and trusted was no longer present for him. However, there was so much else in their relationship of trust, built up over thirty years of marriage, that this was the least of his concerns.

For John, however, this was certainly not the case. He had succeeded, admittedly withstanding a great deal of inner pressure at times, in keeping to the religious values he believed in. He had always wanted to keep a sexual relationship for the special partnership of marriage. It was several years before the increasingly obvious struggle with the physical problem of sexual impotence was understood. Enmeshed in the disappointment and frustration of stop-start sex, he felt a failure and only part-man. The physical relationship swung between extremes, from mutual satisfaction when pregnancy was the goal, to unsatisfactory irregular intercourse following his wife's withdrawal from sexual activity.

At the time he was not able to think clearly; unhappiness and frustration clouded his thoughts. He could only conclude from his impotence that something was physically wrong. His wife went along with this view agreeing that, since he was unable to get an erection, even when the opportunity for sex was available, John would be better served getting on with family life and responsibilities. 'You can't want it as much as you think you do,' was her opinion.

Although for both Denise and John their bodies were the location of the pain of loss, their experiences were quite different. The illness which attacked Denise and robbed her of so much control over her body and life had a basic organic source and demanded medical treatment. Many such physical illnesses need to be assessed for stress and anxiety sources, particularly types of cancer and heart complaints. None the less, physically focused medical treatment is an urgent necessity.

For John it was more a case of the body illustrating and illuminating the sense of loss he was experiencing in his emotional life. As a child John had caught an infection that had affected his health for several years. In maturity it still showed up as a scar on his blood cells and prevented him from being a blood donor. Perhaps, he thought, it had left him with other side-effects. Tests showed no evidence of such side-effects. He was reassured but not helped.

When John entered into a relationship with a second woman he was surprised to find he could easily and wholeheartedly respond to physical and emotional warmth, and was quickly able to enjoy shared affection. The decision that led to renewed physical freedom from apparent limitations incurred losses of a very different nature. Despite the loss of a first marriage relationship, two children, an expected form of family life and struggle with faith and values, the regaining of physical virility and a confidence in his masculinity left John with no regrets.

John's case is by no means unique. Physical symptoms or actual physical illness are all too often a response to experiences of loss. Because they are unable or unwilling to grieve, sufferers leave the body to carry the burden.

The Mind and the Emotions

In any one day the mind and the emotions take as much of a battering as the body. Sit back for a moment and reflect on the past twenty-four hours. Has it been an 'up' or 'down' day? Perhaps it has been both – several times over. Maybe no real traumas, but just switching on the news can send your emotions into orbit. Catching a train or driving to work, going to collect a pension, arranging for then awaiting the late arrival of a plumber – all these and very many other normal daily occurrences can leave us 'drained', 'washed out' or a 'total wreck'.

Having their dog Ritchie put down was, for Andy and Claire, an emotional loss. For Andy it was 'the saddest day of my life'. The sadness re-occurred for Claire each time she went for a walk or drove her car, since Ritchie had always previously accompanied her. Feelings connected with having or losing pets are a potent source of a wider range of responses. But very often we are inhibited from showing grief over our pets because others will think we are 'making a fuss about nothing important'. Some time after Ritchie died Claire said: 'It was very therapeutic to talk about Ritchie, but it wasn't so easy. Unless people know your dog personally, very few understand. They just think "it's only a dog; you can easily get another one", so there's no outlet for your feelings.'

Ritchie was buried alongside several other pets. Claire planted snowdrops and daffodils over the graves and a rosemary bush where a favourite cat was buried. When the possibility of moving house arose, Claire said: 'I didn't like the thought of just leaving them there – of nobody knowing about them anymore. Then I got the idea of making small headstones and painting on a few words about each pet.'

Attachment to our pets arouses all the same kinds of emotions that we feel for our human friends. For old people, in particular, pets are a lifeline: it is now recognized that people who live alone and have a pet as a companion, are likely to live longer. The charity Pets As Therapy runs the PAT Dog scheme whereby volunteers – all members of the PRO Dogs charity – regularly take their canine companions to visit hospitals, hospices and residential homes. The friendly dog and his owner are the only visitors some long-term patients have. On occasions, it has even been requested that the dog lie quietly and comfortably to see out the last moment of a person's life.

Robert's illness was physical but it also led to great emotional loss. The severity of his illness dawned only gradually for this young couple. But once they had accepted the fact of his terminal condition, they made every possible effort to use each minute of their time together. Annette and Robert felt alternately optimistic or despairing, together and with their families. One day they might individually, or as a pair, dismiss the unwelcome reality. 'I am quite sure that Robert will recover; we are just taking precautions by getting married sooner than we had planned,' was Annette's comment on one occasion. Robert had been unwell after chemotherapy that particular day and was unable to attend a wedding preparation meeting at the church. Despite this, a part of Annette still hoped for the best.

In a hospice, a few days before Robert died, the vicar was discussing Robert's choice of hymns for the funeral service. As the vicar left Robert's last words were: 'I can feel myself getting better, I don't think we are going to need that service after all.'

At one and the same time there was acceptance and denial; one moment Robert would be the one to encourage Annette along and gently confront the nearness of the end of his life. On another occasion the roles would be reversed and Annette would confront their dashed hopes of having children together, of enjoying the home they had worked so hard for, of getting old together.

When the end did come, despite the fact it was completely expected and so thoroughly prepared for, Annette's distress was no less deep and shattering. But just as the time spent in preparing for their short life together had been well thought out, so too had Annette's future. She had lost a 'dreamed for' family life but had a 'planned for' future career. Robert had been the man in Annette's life and she never married again. Instead, she put all her creative energies into developing a successful business.

The power of emotion to knock anyone sideways is beyond dispute. But this does not have to mean that the mind shuts up shop and places a 'closed' notice on the door. Losing the job she felt she deserved hurt Lynda badly. The injustice and ingratitude was hard to accept. Could she have done anything differently? Should she have been more 'pushy' and stated her case more directly? Was it really her own fault after all? The shock of disappointment left her feeling 'dead', all her thoughts and feelings were locked away inside. It is not only men who find it impossible to express grief in tears; Lynda, like many other women, felt impelled to keep herself 'under control'. We look at this aspect of her story later, in chapter 4.

In her subsequent battle to resolve the crisis Lynda plummetted to despair and soared to heights of rage and hatred for the new appointee. It disturbed her that she felt such extremes of emotion, and she was aware that she could not continue to live and work in such a state. Eventually, through talking with her new boss, she realised that the new appointee, too, had uncertain feelings in this most uncomfortable situation. In today's business-orientated and increasingly competitive working environment, where company managements constantly place their employees in fraught, no-win circumstances, this is not an unusual scenario. Likewise other social environments, such as schools or clubs, can all create conditions for great highs and lows around fear of failure or hopes of success.

The Spirit

The spiritual dimension is all too often overlooked, misunderstood or ignored altogether. It is discounted by those who see no place in the modern world for belief in, what they perceive as, a 'discredited and outdated concept'. It is all right for those who are sufficiently weak or gullible, they think, but it cannot be given credence by the vast majority of people. In addition, the spiritual dimension is regularly misrepresented because it is positioned only in the realms of the religious; it concerns only thoughts and feelings about a God. However, the need for a sense of meaning and purpose in life is common to so many of us. We may not consider ourselves to be 'religious' but a spiritual need is as present as the need to eat or drink.

Alex had many conflicting influences in her life. The family and Church teaching throughout her childhood and teens; her husband and her children; her personal experiences and inner searching for a balanced view. All these influences affected her grip on her Catholic faith. When she eventually gave it all up she was left with a deep void. A faith taught from childhood remains in the heart, even when the intellect has abandoned its principles and demands. One woman said recently: 'Although I have not been to church for thirty years, when I am dying I shall send for the priest. I am afraid that all I was taught about hell may be true!'

Alex, at sixty, had thought through life and all its vagaries. She was a moral and genuinely compassionate kind of woman and she had a code of values which brought her satisfaction and hope. Her loss was not so much the loss of a belief system – it was the loss of an opportunity to verbally express her deepest worries and conflicts without fear of repercussions. The impersonal confessional had offered a way to confront her inner struggles. The very act of voicing her thoughts and fears aloud had been an enormously positive force in her life.

The depression that constantly dogged her afterwards inevitably had other strands attached. She felt guilty. She felt angry at the injustices perpetrated by an institution that talks so much about love. She worried about her age and present life situation. What might have been a comfort and inspiration at this stage of her life suddenly had no power to offer such support.

Grace was in a similar position in that she, too, was looking for purpose and meaning in her life. It had taken strength of character to claw her way out of a depressed area of London in the 1920s and 30s. She struggled to get training after her Forces service in the war years, and to bring up a family. Later she helped support an older husband. Nothing daunted her as she pushed and wrestled with every new obstacle in her path. But, with mind intact at the age of seventy, questions began to arise. Why have I worked so hard and to what end? Is anyone the better for all my efforts? What is the point of carrying on?

We have many delusions about older age. We expect that worries will suddenly dissolve with increased wisdom, that real problems will diminish. But ageing can bring all these questions to the surface. We start to question a past that is lost for ever; we begin to wonder what might have been done better – and what we ought to have achieved. Such inner turmoil raises the same kinds of feelings which might have been raised by missed opportunities at an earlier stage of life, such as a failed examination. The difference is that now the examination cannot be retaken.

We may have a laugh at those who go round 'navel gazing' but old age can easily force us to question the whole meaning of existence itself. With or without belief in a divine presence, this is a question bearing upon the spiritual dimension to life.

Together with multitudes of older – and younger – people, Alex and Grace continue to wrestle with their struggles, reflective thoughts and former conflicts. But they, like another elderly lady who spoke recently about her life, may be able to find a resolution. She was sipping coffee in a small restaurant with her son as she looked back over her eighty-five years. It was a mild, early summer day and they reminisced about his early childhood as well as her own life. After a moments' silence she looked up and said, 'I would have made all kinds of different decisions in my life – if I had known how things were going to turn out. But I didn't know at the time and now, I am glad that I didn't. But I am tired and I've had enough and I feel I can die without any serious regrets. I don't think I shall see another Christmas.' Three months later she unexpectedly died quickly and peacefully in her own bed.

Body, Mind, and Spirit

The closure of Saltwood Hospital illustrated all the aspects of loss in one hugely disruptive situation, shared by a whole community. A whole range of physical losses resulted from the upheaval of closure, manifesting themselves in actual illness or death. Then there was the loss of place of work and community.

The emotional and mental anguish was encapsulated in the behaviour of Danny, just one patient in the new residence. Each day he toured the new hospital, opening all the doors and asking, 'I'm lost, can you tell me where I can find the chapel?' It was discovered that this particular man had a girlfriend who had moved elsewhere. In the former hospital, the chapel was the place where they used to meet.

Patients and staff alike had been robbed of a way of life to which they had been attached, and which had given their lives a sense of purpose and meaning. The only place that this loss could be shared and the community could grieve was in the chapel of the new hospital. When a patient from the old hospital died, all the former colleagues – nurses, doctors, psychologists, porters and domestics – came to share in the ritual of mourning – this time in the chapel of the new hospital. One of the biggest gatherings of all was the funeral service for Danny.

CHAPTER 3

Who Grieves and How?

Our attitudes to the whole cycle of death, loss and grieving were once quite different to how they are today. A fascinating exhibition, which set out to place grief in a historical context, was recently held in the Victoria and Albert Museum, London. Called 'The Art of Death', it clearly illustrated how attitudes to grief have developed. Just as attitudes to work, sex, family life or the role of women in society have changed dramatically over the years, so has our perspective on grief and mourning.

In an earlier period of our history, the inevitability of death was not seen as a tragedy – it was not even seen as an aspect of life to be kept hidden away. It was woven into the total experience of the journey through life. The route from birth to death was a path; once the first step had been taken, then the moment would arrive for the final step off. Life and death were seen as a seamless garment. The garment would be put on at birth and then, at the appointed time, be finally removed.

More important was the belief that all the intervening experiences from the moment of birth could be used as a preparation for the journey's end. As Nigel Llewellyn points out in his book *The Art of Death*, published to coincide with the exhibition, constant reminders – or 'signposts' – were available. Embroidered tapestries, religious pictures – even jewellery and personal belongings such as snuff boxes, ceramic plates and fans – all boldly displayed the subject of death as their decorative theme.

On the path of a 'good life' it was essential to 'get prepared' for the end which, in turn, made possible a 'good death'. Even those viewed at the time as 'undeserving', such as criminals or traitors, were allowed time to prepare to 'meet their maker' before execution. The very worst kind of end for any mortal man was an unexpected death. By far the most feared in this category was the unmarked death, when the physical whereabouts of the human remains were not known.

Attitudes such as these live on today. There are some who fear cremation, for example. If there are no actual remains, then maybe nothing of the person is available to reap the rewards of eternal life. We have all heard of the concern in America among families and friends of the servicemen who disappeared in Vietnam. Until they are either traced alive or their remains can be given a proper burial, it will be hard for those families to find any peace of mind. The Tomb of the Unknown Warrior in Westminster Abbey has provided a nation, as well as individual mourners, with a place with which they can identify. This marks the passing of one unknown human life as well as a whole generation of soldiers.

Even this may not have satisfied either the hopes or the fears of very many families. Recently I spoke to a Welsh lady who told me about her father's lifelong grief. Her eldest brother was reported missing and nothing else was ever heard of his whereabouts. Her father never got over it. Though they were a large family, with thirteen children, no one was ever left in doubt that the eldest son was the most important member of the family. Each year as Armistice Day approached, their father would become increasingly depressed, and he never changed though he lived into his eighties. Astonishingly enough, he actually died on 11 November – Armistice Day.

Historically, 'good dying' meant more than just a 'resting place' for final remains; the occasion had to be appropriately marked. The establishment of 'ritual' helped mourners express their grief openly and publicly, in a socially acceptable manner, rather than in a lonely, solitary and reclusive way. Certain types of dress and particular types of behaviour showed respect for the deceased. Religious services and established periods of time also assisted in marking the 'passing'. A framework of public and private mourning customs and conventions surrounded the whole business. Outside the home, these rituals demonstrated the prestige and achievements of the deceased, and the social position of his or her family. Only the rituals within the home were aimed at bringing comfort to the mourner.

LIVING FOR NOW

Given that there was an effective and well-tried means of coping with death and loss, how did these customs, which had lasted for centuries, become virtually extinct?

Much of it has to do with the demise of the Church. We have to travel back through history for a moment.

It has been suggested that the customs and beliefs surrounding death changed at the time of the Reformation. The new Church of England, the 'reformed faith', brought with it the assurance of forgiveness right now – rather than having to wait for it until death and risk the uncertainties of Purgatory. One positive contribution that had arisen from the role of Purgatory was the idea that this world could be connected to the After Life. Purgatory was rather like a bridge, or an other-worldly 'sorting office', deciding which souls were deemed worthy enough to continue into the After Life. Suddenly, that all-important stepping stone, that intermediate obstacle course between earthly struggle and heavenly bliss, lost credibility.

To the consternation of a corrupt clergy and a Church with entrepreneurial ambitions, the sale of indulgences also became subject to a recession. Indulgences were religious trinkets, sold by the Church and described as, for example, 'holy water' or bits of 'saints' bones'. These were designed to act as little 'passports' to help people negotiate their way through the moral maze to Paradise.

The new Protestant faith and work ethic emphasized the gift

of life, here and now, in all its richness. In *The Art of Death*, Nigel Llewellyn illustrates how this also paved the way for a distancing of what happens in the 'here and now' from what will happen in the 'there and then'. Because the gap between earth and heaven was widened, society lost touch with After Life, death and, subsequently grieving rituals.

In addition, much time and money were needed to fulfil traditional patterns of mourning. Instead of several changes of outfit to wear on different occasions with a range of colours signifying certain stages in the mourning ritual, a small black muff or scarf or a simple piece of black ribbon attached to a sleeve or hat became a sufficient mark of respect. Six months of retreat from normal social life or, in the case of a widow who belonged to the gentry, a period of years in purdah, could simply not be accommodated as demands from family and work increased.

By the late twentieth century there are few, if any, rites or ceremonies still being observed. The wearing of the traditional black is a thing of the past. At a funeral you are just as likely to be sitting next to someone in a patterned woolly sweater or a coloured anorak. Only members of the older generation would now draw the curtains in their front room if a neighbour or relative had died. Oddly enough though, footballers and other sportsmen still commemorate the occasion of a particularly poignant loss by wearing black armbands.

Although the sight of a black hearse on the road still has the power to cause nippy drivers to slow down and perhaps refrain from their usual practice of intimidating the driver in front by travelling an inch from their bumper, they are relieved to be able to overtake at the first opportunity. The hearse is now more a source of frustration than respect on the road and the sooner it is out of the way the better. Gone are the days of standing quietly to let the hearse go by, removing the hat and bowing the head out of respect – even for a stranger.

Many people were glad to see the back of these mourning rituals. They found the wearing of black depressing and the length of mourning restrictive. They simply wanted to put loss behind them and get on with the business of living. Who could blame them? Trouble is, there's another side to the loss of these rituals: they are lost to society as a whole. Present generations have few means of expressing feelings created by the ever-increasing pressures and varieties of loss.

Where once there was a significant centre of belief in the 'divine', faith is now discounted. Is there any kind of meaningful path through life or are we on a journey to nowhere?

As a consequence of all this, on the surface at least, the response to loss has been polarized. At the one extreme it can take on a much greater sense of inconsolable tragedy. At the other end of the scale it may be viewed as 'no big deal' – at best an embarrassment and at worst a pollutant.

I recently came across examples of these two extremes – the traditional God-fearing and the rational atheistic view – in a hospital setting. Mrs S, who was in her eighties, explained that she had only become confirmed after the death of her husband. She said:

> He served for twenty-two years in the Guards and then, when he retired, we set up our own business. His faith meant everything to him and I envied the strength he seemed to find from taking communion. He died at forty-seven and not a day has passed without me thinking of him. Without the faith I learned from him I would not have brought up our children or survived in the business. Taking communion gives me strength; it also brings me closer to my husband. When I die, then I shall be with him again.

Mr J was 103 years of age and, although physically frail, he still had a keen sense of humour and a razor-sharp mind. When I introduced myself, as hospital chaplain, Mr J smiled pleasantly adding, 'I am very pleased to see you – as long as you do not intend to talk about religion.' We had a thoroughly enjoyable half-hour's conversation, during which Mr J explained:

> I was a young subaltern during the Great War. Any religious beliefs that I took with me into the Army were soon knocked out of me by the horrors and the carnage of it all. I have lived without God from that time very happily; I intend to

die without him too. We live, we die and that's the end of it.

Such sentiments have a pretty good pedigree. Shakespeare has Macbeth voicing such thoughts:

> Out, out brief candle.
> Life's but a walking shadow, a poor player
> That struts and frets his hour upon the stage,
> And then is heard no more. It is a tale
> told by an idiot, full of sound and fury,
> Signifying nothing

A comparable view seems to be expressed in the Old Testament Jewish book of Psalms:

> All mortals are like grass;
> All their splendours like the flower of the field;
> The grass withers, the flowers fall;
> But (and only) the word of the Lord endures for ever.

Despite the fact that Mr J has come to terms with his mortality and faces his own death with no apparent anxiety, there will be many who will mourn his passing: relatives, friends, community nurses and hospital staff – all of whom have valued him as a person. There will also be a sense of loss at the passing of someone whose personal history and experience is unique.

Not everyone can retain the sense of meaning and purpose that faith and a hope for reunion with a loved one can bring, as it did for Mrs S. On the other hand, those with the confidence of Mr J do not always survive and then prepare for death with a conviction like his. Most of us lie somewhere in between – seeking reassurance for the future and comfort for the present.

LOSS, RELIGION AND CULTURE

Comfort for the present is often hard to find, especially in an age of increasing violence and hardship which is brought nearer through the development of world news coverage. I remember seeing a television news programme where, after an air disaster, the victims were being taken home to Italy in coffins. On arrival, they were met at the airport by friends and relatives who threw themselves bodily over the coffins and sobbed with total abandon. Indeed, I recall watching this particular news item with a British friend who was frankly amazed at such 'an exhibition' and simply found the whole thing beyond comprehension.

Because of such coverage of world events it is easy to observe how other nationalities openly express their anger and sorrow. We have all watched harrowing pictures from war zones or areas of natural disaster showing weeping fathers carrying dead infants in their arms, or distraught elderly women waving photographs of family members who have been killed in fighting or – perhaps worse – are still missing.

There was a time when as soon as anyone opened his or her mouth to speak it was easy to tell where they had come from. Even if an Irishman or a Geordie had lived in Wales or Sussex for fifty years, he or she would continue to be easily identifiable. The same might be said of a Cockney, a Mancunian, or a miner from the Midlands. Although, thankfully, there are still some differences and identity attached to regional origins, these are being eroded. The increasing population shift and inroads made by mass culture has affected regional variations in accent, language and customs. Mass media, chain store development and architectural styles now spread uniformly over the UK, squeezing out local and individual characteristics as they grow. Today the range of differences is far narrower.

In the same way that accents, words or expressions might once have easily identified us, so also might our customs attached to grieving. To some degree they can still identify our regions of origin or our cultural and religious heritage. The British people have developed a whole variety of ways to commemorate the passing of a loved one – normally embedded in regional religious persuasions.

Ireland, as well as some parts of Northern England, is famous for its 'wakes'. These enthusiastic family gatherings have traditionally provided the opportunity to share loss, offer comfort and then make a party of the whole affair. Even into the late

1970s it would have been the norm for an Irish 'wake' to have lasted for two nights and three days. An elderly woman might have been wrapped in a Legion of Mary shroud, to hallow her passing. It was usual to cover mirrors with a white cloth; the fires would have been doused and all the clocks would have been stopped.

Today, the funeral parlour has taken over from the front parlour. Congregations in the Pentecostal Church, celebrate the transition from this life to a better one with great exuberance and enthusiasm. The Society of Friends – or Quakers as they are sometimes known – simply and silently reflect on the life of the deceased. This, in turn, is in total contrast to the scale and complexity of a Requiem Mass.

Although all these farewell ceremonies continue, it is much more usual to experience the more 'clinical' confines of the crematorium. What some would describe as a rather impersonal – and rapid – point of departure is perfectly acceptable for very many people. Even when the genuine kindness and consideration of the staff at many a crematorium or undertakers could not be faulted, there is often a rather 'mechanical' feel to the occasion.

The speed and efficiency surrounding this final farewell provides little time and few ritual symbols for our grief – all quite a contrast to the wake! Instead of the final scene in the traditional burial ceremony of watching the coffin being lowered into the ground, with the words 'earth to earth, ashes to ashes . . .', the crematorium service involves an intermediate stage where the coffin discreetly slips away between closing curtains, and is then removed to the incinerator for disposal. After a cremation ceremony mourners are more likely to spend a subdued and uncomfortable few minutes trying to compose themselves around the display of flowers at the back of the crematorium. At the very heart of this grief event, there is neither the time for nor the means with which to grieve. When it comes to different races, cultures and faiths, then the range of responses to loss is even broader and deeper.

DOING THINGS DIFFERENTLY

When the Nationalist Army fled from China to Formosa, as the island of Taiwan was then known, it took with it many of the customs of old China. Although Taiwan is very much in tune with the modern twentieth century, it still retains many of those ancient Chinese practices. They have been both fascinating and bemusing Westerners since the days of Marco Polo.

One of the first sights that I remember in Taiwan was that of a traditional funeral procession on its way to the cemetery. A highly decorative and colourful bullock-drawn cart carried an ornate coffin with spectacular brass fittings. It looked just like a float on its way to a carnival. This tinsel 'house' was, in fact, the family offering. The sculpted paper articles within symbolized what the deceased would need in the next life. Following this cart were around twenty adults and children with what looked like old sacks tied around their bodies and sacking hoods over their heads. I learned that these mourners were not family members, or even friends; they were professional mourners who had been paid to weep, wail and show the family sorrow. As it was not 'socially acceptable' for Orientals to publicly express their grief, those who were rich enough paid someone else to do it for them. The numbers of those dressed in sackcloth and ashes indicated the wealth and position of both the deceased and the family.

When I arrived in Taipei, to my surprise, the Bishop was at the airport to greet me. This jolly, humorous and extremely wealthy man, who had made his fortune in shipping, had on retirement decided to become ordained and was immediately promoted to the top church post in Taiwan. Some months later I attended a morning service at St John's Cathedral in Taipei. The young priest who was the Bishop's Chaplain hurried into the service rather late, then joined us for coffee afterwards. He had served under the Bishop for several years and was known to greatly respect and admire him. Suddenly, with a deep and broad smile, this young man announced the news: 'The Bishop has died.' My Mandarin wasn't all that sound at the time and I thought that I must have misheard him – after all, the bad news and the broad grin did not appear to go together. He repeated his news: 'The Bishop is dead', and then, in growing confusion, hurried off.

Although he had been educated in the West, this priest was fundamentally Oriental and could not possibly express his grief in a public setting. His smile was just as much an outer covering, a defence against the stares of onlookers, as was the hired wailing of the professional mourners at the funeral procession. Ancient Confucian or Taoist practices were just as central to the make-up of a Christian priest, despite Western influence.

A Chinese family gathering to mark a death in the family can last over three days and has much in common with an Irish wake. Even among the present-day, multi-storey, high-rise apart-ment blocks of Singapore and Hong Kong, the 'wake equivalent' continues. Any available patch of land between the flats becomes a tented encampment where family, friends and acquaintances gather to sympathize, eat, drink and gamble away the days and nights of the next seventy-two hours. Whereas that young priest was steeped in his Oriental heritage, many other young Chinese have nearly lost all knowledge of or sympathy for their ancient rituals.

It is now perfectly possible to have wide cultural differences in the same family. This can introduce other kinds of losses, as in the case of one young Chinese man. When he was an eighteen-month-old baby, DAVID had contracted polio and the next five years of his life were spent in hospital with only short visits home. Since David's home was a long way from the hospital, family visits were few. His mother spoke only an ancient Chinese dialect, Techew. In the hospital, David learned English from his nurses. When he finally returned home, he worked hard to learn Mandarin but could never master more than a few words of Techew. Needless to say, communication between David and his mother could only ever be very basic and their relationship was almost non-existent.

When she was eventually taken very ill, David tried to show his concern in practical ways but couldn't actually talk to her. When she died David was filled with remorse and guilt that he hadn't made more of an effort to get to know her. Although he had by then lived for many years under the same roof as his mother, she was sadly little more than a stranger to him.

Cultural differences are, of course, especially evident among first and second generation immigrants to Britain. All too often the divide that exists between these generations widens to a chasm and, what gradually evolved over decades in the West has happened for them in a single generation. The loss which results from unresolved parent-children relationships is illustrated by a Sikh family.

MIRANDER decided to train as a nurse. Her parents were proud of her ability, yet they decided to try to dissuade her. When it became clear to them that Mirander's mind could not be altered, they allowed her to train but never asked about her progress. The only time they even acknowledged their daughter's training was when they enquired about when her training would be completed. With determined resolve they set about finding her a suitable husband. In her final year of training, each time Mirander returned to see her parents she found a new man who had been invited to the home to meet her.

Then her father was taken ill and, on returning home to visit him, Mirander found herself confronted with a 'deathbed request'. Her father asked that now, since she was qualified, she should give up her nursing to marry and bring grandchildren into the family. At great risk to her own future peace of mind, as well as the likelihood of complete rejection by her family, Mirander turned down the request.

Today, Mirander continues to nurse and her father continues to get ill. She gets very anxious about the future and feels both manipulated and terribly lonely at the same time. In addition to this, she now lives with a young Catholic man, but, naturally, would not dream of telling her family about him.

Alongside this very personal battle that is taking place between a father and his daughter, is the clash between two cultures. It is easy for an outsider to make judgements about the 'rights and wrongs' of such a clash. From the family point of view it is a battle for the survival of the culture. From Mirander's perspective, however, it is her future and her right to make her own decisions that is at stake. What has already been lost from the

Irish or North of England culture, the Jew, the Sikh or the Muslim is seeking to preserve in his. It may be a battle against change, or simply to limit the effects of change, but it is also a determined attempt to prevent losing a valuable community means of caring and support for its members.

Whether in times of celebration or, more especially, at times of grieving, ritual supports which have been largely lost to twentieth-century Britons are still available to people of other cultures. The traditional Sikh expresses his belief in life and at death by wearing the five 'Ks', which must never be removed. The *Kesh* – or hair – is always kept long; a *Kangha* is a small comb which is worn in the hair at all times; the *Kara* steel bracelet or ring is worn on the right wrist; the *Kachha* is a type of under garment; the *Kirpaan* a small sword. There are specific rituals prior to and during a Sikh funeral and, a year after the deceased has passed away, family and friends will gather to pray, sing hymns and to give to charity.

Hindus believe in one God and also in rebirth. A 'good death' for a Hindu and the hope of a good 'Karma' or next life continues to be of the greatest importance. This can be helped by offering food and other articles to the needy or to the Temple, before death. The symbolic offer of a female calf, made out of Kusha grass, ensures a safe passage in the short journey to the next incarnation. Ganges water and the leaves of the sacred Tulsi plant complete the necessary contributions to speed the dying Hindu on his or her way. Thirteen days of mourning are allowed, to ensure that the family are given time to grieve and are properly supported.

The Buddhist also places great significance on the experience of dying. Here the vital aspect is not artefacts but information about the time of death. The Buddhist, who believes in the act of 'Puja' or worship rather than God, will wish to prepare appropriately in his mind for the end, wishing to be both positive and conscious of all that is happening. Rebirth into the next life will depend on the actions of the believer in this one. Death itself holds few fears for the Buddhist. The Buddhist follows an eightfold path through life: understanding life, having the right motives, the right speech, conduct, livelihood, self-discipline, right mindedness and meditation. Providing this path has been followed correctly, then the quality of the next life will be ensured.

The Muslim faces Mecca in his daily prayer ritual. At the time of death facing Mecca is a comfort and reassurance, both to the believer and his relatives and friends. The extended family and community play an important part in providing comfort and support.

In Judaism, while there is the hope of an After Life – either in the resurrection of the body or a spiritual existence – it's the present, earthly life that is of prime importance. There are the rituals of prayer but the process of dying is seen as a personal event which may be best met alone.

Wakes and other death and funeral rituals have an important part to play and, at the time, are a good way of helping ease initial shock. But it is important to keep these differing attitudes to death, as well as the accompanying rituals and rites, in perspective. They are of great value in those initial stages of the grieving process.

But, having recovered from the initial trauma , the rest of the painful feelings will need to be faced and – hopefully – resolved. Don't imagine that specific cultural and religious responses are some sort of panacea.

LOSS AND HELPLESSNESS

Some of us grieve over situations that we are not directly connected with or are far removed from our daily lives, about which it's unlikely we can do much. We can become upset, gloomy and often extremely angry about events which are out of our daily realm. There is no reason why others should understand why we feel so strongly about something we have read in the newspaper that day or heard about on the radio, so we try to push our feelings down, put on a 'normal' face for the day ahead, and press on. In its own particular way, this is also an experience of loss – the loss of control or influence.

Cruelty to animals is one issue which never fails to upset me. It may be an individual who has just received a meagre fine for an appalling act, or a legal cruelty like dancing bears in Eastern Europe, or a lorry load of beagles suffocating to death while on their way from Britain to be vivisected in Scandinavia.

Then there are the newspaper reports of elderly people being terrorized for years before being murdered by their own neighbours. You learn that they first tried to seek help for themselves by going through the 'right' channels – complaining to the council, informing the police and then their MPs – all to no avail.

The callous murder of a small boy who was lured away from his parents caused an entire nation to mourn. The horrifying killing of an elderly woman who was bullied for years then strangled with a dog lead in her own home resulted in angry public demonstrations.

Organized, formal grieving rituals may be more scarce now but 'grass roots' improvised public demonstrations of grief are appearing more and more often. Witness the number of floral tributes that are now placed by the roadside at the scene of a terrorist bombing or a fatal motor accident. When we lived in London the singer and musician Marc Bolan was killed in a car accident at the end of our road. Now, years later, bouquets, handwritten notes and other home-fashioned tributes are still to be found pinned to the tree where he died.

The Hillsborough football stadium tragedy gave rise to a huge display of community grief. The mountain of bouquets placed at the scene by individuals and the successive queues of people who filed past to pay their respects were followed by a vast public memorial service. You don't have to be directly involved in a tragedy to feel the need to share the grief. Numbers of memorial services seem to be growing. Whether they are for celebrities, the influential or just well-loved friends and valued members of the community, these services offer the opportunity for the deceased to live on in some way.

IN LOVING MEMORY

There are many more individual and personal ways in which we can commemorate a loss and give pleasure to the living at the same time. Parks and seafronts the length of the land are lined with wooden benches bearing small tributes to deceased loved ones. Donated by those who are left behind, they also add to the pleasure of people in the local community.

Planting a tree or shrub is another way in which a 'living memorial' can mark a loss. Just before she died, my mother-in-law gave me a lovely red-stemmed winter shrub for my birthday. When we moved house, it was still small enough to be dug up and replanted in our new garden. Several new bushes are now growing from the cuttings.

In chapter 2 we related how Andy and Claire planted flowers over their pets' graves in the back garden. These days, if you have a pet put down at the vets, it is not always lawfully possible to take the body home with you. However, the charity PRO Dogs is planning a memorial garden at its Kent headquarters where people will have the opportunity to donate a shrub in memory of their pet. PRO Dogs also highlights another way to offer a memorial: occasionally someone meets the financial cost of producing an information leaflet, in memory of their dog.

Paying for something useful and practical doesn't have to mean anything as grand as a new hospital wing. It could mean something far more modest. A charity leaflet, a children's playground swing or an annual outing for a group of people normally confined to a home or institution would make an imaginative, fitting and, for others, welcome tribute to a lost friend or relative.

CHAPTER 4

Why am I Afraid?

Grief is a perfectly natural response to the inevitable experiences of life, and yet many of us – perhaps without realizing it – are scared to grieve. The ancient Greek philosopher Seneca, writing to a young friend about being too ambitious, suggested that if all he was concerned about was coming first then: 'You will judge death to be the greatest of evils, though there is nothing evil in death, except what precedes it – our fears of it.'

In trying to get on with his life after loss, C. S. Lewis, writing a diary in which he observed his own grief, wrote: 'No one ever told me that grief felt so like fear. I am not afraid, but the sensation is like being afraid. The same fluttering in the stomach, the same restlessness, the yawning. I keep on swallowing . . .' Speaking from his own very moving personal experience he was right to say that his feeling just appeared in the guise of fear. We suspect that, for many of us, fear is actually quite real and definite.

Remembering that anger is one important component of grief, I recall something I was told many years ago: 'The two basic human emotions are rage and fear. Where one is particularly apparent, be sure that the other is lurking in its shadow.'

But just what is it we are afraid of?

Many of us have been brought up to 'be brave' and 'keep a stiff upper lip' and expressive grieving goes against all we have learned. Others will fear the reactions of those around them. Friends, family and acquaintances may be shocked by weeping, anger and generally 'going to pieces'; they might think us immature or 'unmanly'. Then there is the issue of change. The majority of us do not welcome change because of our fear of the unknown and what it might bring. Sometimes it is a whole lot easier to push the prospect of grieving to one side and hope the whole business will disappear. Much easier, we may suppose, than facing up to what could be a painful experience. It could be that grieving, for some of us, means confronting issues from the past that we would rather not think about. The reasons for not grieving are many and varied. Identifying and examining possible reasons for our fears may help us confront the grieving process.

BEING 'BRAVE'

In chapter 2 we looked at the experience of Lynda, a woman in her early forties who failed to secure the job she had aimed and toiled for all her working life. She said that losing it was the biggest disappointment of her life and that a lot of anger and bitterness followed the initial hurt. When she received the news, by telephone, that someone else had been offered the job and had accepted, Lynda said: 'I felt winded. After I put the phone down one tear trickled down my cheek, but I didn't cry. I just sat staring out of the window for most of that afternoon.'

The anger and resentment hadn't set in at first. 'I just felt dead', she said. Lynda explained that she hadn't wanted to talk about it with anyone – family, friends or colleagues, that she had 'put on an act'. Looking back she felt that if she had shown she was really upset – expressed her grief openly, then she wouldn't have been so angry for so long.

With hindsight, Lynda realized that her first reactions to her loss were all about 'keeping control' of her feelings. She was able to link this with the long period that she spent in hospital when, as a child, she was seriously ill. 'Be brave' was the advice she was given and this she equated with not crying. But in actual fact, when the job-loss situation arose, Lynda was not 'keeping control' at all, quite the opposite. She wasn't sobbing over her desk and telling her husband and friends all about her upset but she was harbouring increasingly angry and bitter thoughts towards her work and colleagues. As one set of emotions were suppressed, another set of different emotions bobbed up. We don't know what would have happened if Lynda had spent the afternoon weeping after that telephone call. What we do know is that initially she tried to 'keep control' and only later came to realize that 'being brave' is not always about hiding emotions or trying to show you don't care.

BE A MAN

Men are often accused of not communicating when something upsets them and, instead, becoming very withdrawn. But Lynda, too, confused 'being brave' with 'not crying'. It would probably be a mistake therefore to think that the difficulties confronting men are unique to them. However, it is generally accepted that men find it harder to show their true feelings than women, and that they are probably less inclined to discuss their feelings and emotions with friends or spouses, electing instead to keep things to themselves. Perhaps this is because they are concerned about demonstrating what they perceive as weakness or lack of courage. Many men are brought up to be 'tough'. Either way, it can create very real problems.

SEAN is a bereavement counsellor and former nurse who has had his own share of losses. His father died when he was nine; his mother died on his sixteenth birthday; his wife died about five years ago. From his own personal observations as a counsellor, Sean is certain that from a very young age men are socially conditioned not to cry. 'There are very few men who grieve in a conventional way,' he says. 'Instead, they tend to suppress their grief and do nothing with it. They can't be seen to be weak and they rarely cry, so they put on a stiff upper lip and "get on with it".' Sean has seen bereaved men who either remarry very quickly because they are reluctant to live by themselves, who throw themselves into the lives of their children, or who immerse themselves into one hobby or their work. They appear to follow a single track and, in doing so, feel no need to 'do' anything with their grief because they are too busy; they haven't the time to think about it.

Sean believes that men operate differently from women and therefore look at their own losses quite differently. He says that, as a counsellor, he sees about three times more women than men. Those that are able to shed tears do so, or openly voice their feelings. 'These are the ones counsellors can most fully work with,' Sean explains. In marriage counselling and in cases of loss already experienced, men either don't come forward for help or fail to turn up as arranged. Because women are more forthcoming, the great majority of support given is by women and for women. When Sean's own wife died, even though he was a counsellor, he found that help was thin on the ground. He says:

> I was not a young man with young children; I was not an infirm elderly person; I was working full-time and I was a man. I then discovered that men in my category fall through every hole in the support system. The services that are available seem to be mainly for middle-aged, middle-class women. I was aware of that for a long time.

It took some years for Sean to work through his own grieving process.

WHERE'S YOUR BACKBONE?

The challenge to 'be a man' has traditionally been a call to 'face up to things', to 'show some backbone'. Many of us simply don't expect a cricketer, footballer or any other sportsmen to burst into tears when he is injured or upset at a referee's ruling and, when it does happen, it makes headline news. I can still see in my mind's eye, one eleven-year-old in my house rugby team. Quite legally I 'handed him off' – the palm of my hand hitting him in the face – as he tried to tackle me. He sat down and cried because it had hurt him, and I was so amazed I can remember the incident to this day. I suppose it is the same macho streak in the British spectator that admires the player who continues to play when obviously badly injured. On the other hand, this same macho tendency manifests itself through the abhorrence of the football supporter who is aroused to fury pitch by the histrionic exhibition of a player writhing on the ground when his injury is suspect.

This attitude is not exclusive to us British. Many different cultures seem to encourage an admiration of stalwart male endurance in times of stress. Women as well as men encourage this attitude. When 'putting on a brave front' means suppressing feelings that really ought to be let out, this can lead to deep-rooted emotions that are likely to fester, then surface again – perhaps years later. On the whole, we can accept tears in children and old men, though often we would much prefer that they also refrained from crying, but from the self-respecting male adult – certainly not!

Fortunately these attitudes are, at last, changing. This change is exemplified in the following case of a bereaved father. After yet another terrible bombing, a family had to come to terms with the horror of their youngest son's terrible injuries. Very publicly and with no attempt to hide his feelings the father spoke to the media. The family grief was there for all to see and to share and, I believe, brought its own response of compassionate kindness.

The father also wrote about the experience: the numbing disbelief of the news following a frantic search to discover where the son might be; the distress at encountering the smell of the bomb blast around the bandaged but mortally wounded small body; the flicker of a hope that the practical joker of the family might suddenly jump up and show it was all just another one of his pranks. The father described his decision to stay beside his son to lie on the bed with him when the life-support machine was to be switched off. The staff had warned that there could be a violent bodily reaction but, in the event, the boy died peacefully in his father's arms. The open honesty of all this must have proved an enormous help to many other people.

Confronted by such tragedy, being terribly afraid of both the situation and the dreadful loss would have been excusable. When asked whether he had regretted giving interviews so freely and talking about his emotions, the father said some very important things. He explained that it was not a struggle and that his son had been taken away so violently that he needed to talk about him. It helped as a sort of therapy.

> People have said we have been so dignified. They seem to have put us on a pedestal, which is wrong. We are not made of special stuff. We did it for our son and to mobilize public opinion . . . We did have little time for ourselves during those weeks. I was glad of the activity. But I don't know how I am going to react as time goes on. There's no problem yet, but the real grieving has not yet begun.

At least he and his family's courageous frankness should have benefited them as they pick up the pieces of their lives.

GOING TO PIECES

One of my own regrets is that I find it hard to allow myself to cry at funerals. I've lost some good friends and am sorry that because of my own inhibitions I was not more fully able to take part in their 'goodbye' ceremonies. A few years ago I had two elderly and very great friends – Patricia and Ellen. Patricia had been severely crippled all her life and the medical profession marvelled at the fact she had even reached sixty-five years of age. Despite her great disability she had been in full employment until retirement, and had led a broad and varied life. When Patricia found out she was dying she took great care to sort out all her finances and other affairs and then went into hospital for two weeks before passing away.

Ellen, who was Patricia's friend, was of a similar mould in that she was involved, interested, extraordinarily selfless, enormous fun, took her numerous commitments very seriously, and never, ever complained that she was too busy. An Oxford graduate in Theology, she had taught all her working life. One summer she arranged to meet a Canadian friend for a watercolour painting holiday in the depths of South America and it was there that she discovered she had cancer. It spread very swiftly and everyone was astounded when, very soon after her return to England, she was admitted to hospital and died.

Patricia and Ellen brought interest, fun, entertainment and friendship into the lives of many others. When they died – within a year of each other – a great number of people felt the loss.

Georgina was another friend. She was more of a 'struggler' than Patricia or Ellen. Georgina had lived most of her life with her mother, had worked hard and conscientiously in the 'gowns' department of a smart London store before retiring and eventually going to live in a residential home. She told me she was depressed quite a lot and found it hard to get on with some people. A lifelong Christian, she taught me a lot about prayer.

Both Patricia and Ellen had small, private, family funerals and then memorial services to which their large numbers of friends and acquaintances could be invited. Georgina had a simple funeral, just a few people. I would have liked to weep freely at all three events but, for some reason, couldn't allow myself. The effort of this self-control certainly detracted from the benefit of the services for me. But I regret the fact that I was thinking about myself rather than my friends. As a result, for months afterwards, I found that I could barely refer to any of the individuals in front of other people. I was afraid of 'breaking down' and so, of course, I never really grieved.

Why was I afraid to grieve? It may have stemmed from a fear of confronting reality when I was a child. After my parents split up and my younger sister went to live with my father I have no recollection of grieving, although life was greatly disrupted and changed for ever. Six years later, when I was eleven and my mother went abroad for a year (with air travel so much slower in those days, regular visits were out of the question) I didn't shed one tear. Looking back, this seems an odd reaction for an eleven-year-old. I believe I was simply pushing 'bad' things out of my mind – trying to pretend they weren't happening, or at the very least that they weren't all that important.

Perhaps my fear of crying at funerals is now part of a lifelong habit. Hopefully, since I am now aware of it, I might learn to allow myself to express grief in a more open manner. Perhaps if I wasn't so easily embarrassed about showing grief in public it would be easier - but that probably has more to do with my natural characteristics rather than any previous experiences.

WHAT WILL PEOPLE THINK?

A few weeks after Patricia had died I visited another friend who had known Patricia only slightly. She happened to be entertaining a guest but she invited me in. Drawing me into the conversation she asked by chance, 'And how is Patricia getting on?' Of course she hadn't known that Patricia had died, so I told her, then promptly and spontaneously burst into tears.

I'd like to have had a jolly good cry but realizing that the other two - perhaps understandably - were looking 'extremely uncomfortable' I tried to stop. In the end, when I had 'composed myself', I attempted to get the conversation going again. Naturally enough, they didn't know what to do; and why should they? But it would have been a help to me if they had let me cry and asked a few questions about Patricia. I would have greatly welcomed the opportunity to talk about her and remember some of the times we had shared.

It is always possible that the person grieving their loss would be glad of the chance to speak about it. It is unlikely they will want advice, 'constructive comment' or 'good ideas' about how to pick up the pieces again. Nor will they want the other party to say 'I do understand what you mean' before embarking on their own 'similar' story. They want to voice the thoughts and feelings that are swirling around inside them. Saying things out loud is a great way to clarify a situation and, if someone is kind enough to listen, then we don't feel quite so alone in our distress.

Many people will not know how to respond, for fear of offending or saying the wrong thing, and this will cause them to look uncomfortable. Where grief is connected to death, some will be so scared themselves of death that they simply can't bear to hear about it. Just as the one suffering loss will have all kinds of feelings affecting every part of their lives, so also will the listener respond in a variety of ways.

By understanding that others carry their own emotional 'baggage' we can relax a little and feel less self-conscious when it comes to airing our own feelings. We may also switch off from worrying too much about what others think of us. Wouldn't it be wonderful to be able to stop apologizing and get on with being ourselves?

THE CHALLENGE OF CHANGE

Fear of grieving arising from denial of a situation and failure to accept what is happening could be rooted in dread of change. In chapter 1 we saw how David could not accept the changing circumstances of his job. He was 'moved sideways' into a position with less influence and responsibility but he continued to act as though nothing was different. 'They won't get rid of me that easily' was his response. David had spent many years in his job and, on the face of it, was 'too old' and ill-equipped to adjust to a new life. But the most surprising people dig deep into their inner resources and David's story had a happy ending. After six months of 'resisting change' he accepted the reality of his situation, took early retirement, went on to gain a place at university and fulfilled a long-forgotten dream of gaining a good education.

Perhaps what David was doing was escaping from what business management expert Charles Handy calls 'The "They" Syndrome'. Initially David had said, 'They are not going to get rid of me.' In a few months, however, he was doing something for himself. Charles Handy tells of a wily old Scot who spotted him waiting outside the Personnel Manager's office. 'What are you waiting for, laddie?' he asked. 'I am waiting to see what they are planning for me,' Handy replied. 'Och, invest in yourself my boy, don't wait for them. Invest in yourself; if you don't, why should they?'

I used to work for an international publishing company. Those of us who were employed there were accustomed to dealing with deadlines, last-minute alterations to plans, juggling with budgets, the ups and downs of communication with others. In fact, it was not a lot different to the usual happenings of daily life. We all coped pretty calmly with most of these occurrences.

However, the one issue that guaranteed to put noses out of joint, backs up, cause rows and generally make people feel distraught, insecure and vulnerable was . . . changing the office furniture around. It was more than an issue of territory, personal space, or the means with which we could deal with the practicalities of the working day. It was more even than a measure of our individual worth. Having your desk moved heralded 'Big Change'. Rearranging the work space, we suspected, could well lead to far greater alterations, such as rearranging the staffing structures (you might get a boss you loathed) and reorganization of the pay packets. It might even mean some pay packets could stop altogether – through redundancy. In short, we associated 'change' with things changing for the worse.

Loss is often about change. And if people can get upset about having their office furniture moved around, then the fears attached to losing a loved one or home are clearly enormous. Lose a partner, a job, your health or your faith, and life will never be the same again. The consequences of your loss will be largely unknown; there will be no certainties. It means trying to be prepared for the unexpected and adapting to new circumstances.

In some cases, when the loss is expected, certain plans can be made. When parents realize their children have all grown up and are about to move out of the family home for good, they can prepare for the loss by introducing new interests and commitments into their own lives. They may come to welcome the loss because it will give them more time for other pursuits and responsibilities. When a person knows retirement is approaching or is given warning that they are likely to be made redundant, they at least have the chance to prepare for a drastic change of lifestyle. When the loss hits you like a thunderbolt there is no time to prepare. The changes come hard and fast. Whether it's an expected or an unexpected loss we are still afraid to grieve because we don't want to accept the reality of the situation or face the changes this will bring.

Today we are living in a world of constant change. In this country the job situation means having to uproot and move to completely new and unknown areas, with children having to adapt to new schools. The old 'jobs for life' situation has ceased, which means we may go through several types of job or career and have to retrain more than once. People divorce more than they used to. We live longer and are likely, at some point, to leave the family home for a small flat or residential care, which is devastating for many elderly folk. There are far fewer certainties than there once were and change is now an integral part of life.

Change doesn't have to be for the worse; it may not necessarily be for the better, either. It usually just means doing things differently. It will almost certainly mean fresh opportunities.

FACING THE FACTS

Fear of grieving will, in some cases, be related to unwillingness to face reality. When RUTH'S parents split up her father was awarded custody of the two sisters but it was agreed, through a private arrangement between the parents, that Ruth would stay with her mother while her younger sister JEAN went with her father. The two girls were brought up separately: Jean growing up with a stepmother, two half-sisters and two half-brothers; and Ruth with a stepfather in the family.

Jean's stepmother could never accept the fact that her husband had been previously married. The situation arose whereby Jean's younger half-brothers and sisters were brought up to believe that their mother was also Jean's mother. By this time Ruth's visits to her father's home had been discouraged and then stopped altogether. All traces of the previous marriage, as far as Jean's new family were concerned, had been erased. In the meantime, Ruth grew up in the knowledge that she had lost a father, sister and four half-siblings. She felt conscious of the fact that she was, in effect, a 'secret' daughter and an outcast of her father's family. She did, however, keep in contact with Jean by letter until the sisters grew up and could travel to see each other under their own steam.

Ruth was five and Jean was three when their parents separated and divorced. Ruth never openly grieved about the situation; she can never remember Jean being upset about her circumstances. Although Ruth felt sympathy for Jean who, from a very young age, was having to shoulder the burden of her father and his wife's lie, she tried to accept things as they were and never allowed herself to feel angry with either of her parents for failing to prevent the situation developing. She tried to be 'reasonable' and 'mature' about the whole business and to respect Jean's stepmother's wishes. She even continued, out of a sense of daughterly responsibility, to send birthday and Christmas cards to her father and his second wife.

Forty years on, Ruth now feels deep anger about her childhood circumstances and animosity towards Jean's stepmother. Ruth thinks that if, instead of 'being reasonable' as a child and teen-ager, she had allowed the grieving process to run its course, the feelings of anger and injustice she harbours today would not be there. Looking back she believes she denied the importance of her lost family at the time. She can see now that she didn't want to face a situation that was extremely painful and one that she was powerless to do anything about. Ruth continues to feel haunted by the spectre of what she regards as her 'unnatural' family background. Incidentally, Jean has never married nor had any children and Ruth has been married twice but has not had any children of her own.

It's just possible that 'myths' and 'fairy stories' about 'wicked stepmothers' and 'malicious step-families' have their origins in such situations. The reality is not of wickedness or malicious intentions, but rather of passionate angers, guilt and anxieties that are aroused but are fearfully suppressed. Both women made a personal choice not to have children. This may or may not be something to do with their own experiences as children. For these two sisters denial of grief has proved paralysing. It has contributed to their failure to come to terms with their life situations and to their inability to take stock and then move on into new phases of their lives.

Some people associate 'getting upset' with admitting failure. For example, DON and JUDY sold their comfortable, conventional home, bought an old school in the West Country and, with enthusiasm and energy, set about converting it. Their two-year plan gradually turned into five and still the end was not in sight. Apart from the extra time and effort involved, the project was eating up far more money than they had originally intended. Gradually the couple became more and more despondent; their relationship came under an increasing strain. Neither of them wanted to entertain the idea that their dream was about to collapse and that they would have failed. It did go through their minds that they should have remained in their comfortable, conventional home. This they could not talk about until very much later.

Don and Judy did eventually voice their fears, lament the loss of their former lifestyle, despair of ever getting the new home into any kind of shape. Yes, they did go through a phase of thinking they had made a mistake – but they came out of it. Their old school is now a beautiful home and they've even had time to create a breathtaking garden. The plan simply took much longer and involved more difficulties and setbacks than they had anticipated.

Loss of goals whether they are plans for a new business, hopes for a great career, a wish for a large family – or any family at all, or building your own dream house can have a greatly debilitating effect. Plans don't always work out as originally intended: new businesses fail to get off the ground; not all second marriages turn out happily; hopes, aims and goals slip from our grasp – or were, perhaps, never attainable in the first place. Facing the fact that something hasn't turned out as hoped for, realizing the loss, and eventually grieving over the misfortune gives us the strength to more realistically assess the situation and then move on once again.

AM I GOING MAD?

Loss has a knack of arousing some powerful feelings and it's not uncommon, even, for people to think they are going mad. Because most of us keep a very tight rein on our feelings, when they take us over it is terribly disturbing. We say: 'I'm not usually like this' or 'You must excuse me. I can't understand what has come over me!' Sometimes we apologize: 'How ungrateful of me to be so miserable, when everyone has been so helpful.' We find ourselves repeating these phrases in our own minds and to those around us. Perhaps we are trying to excuse what we see as a weakness in ourselves. Or again we might feel like the widower who told me: 'It was all right to begin with; if I cried when a neighbour spoke to me it didn't matter. But it's six months now and I still cry. I've stopped going out now; I really don't want to embarrass anyone else.'

Whatever the reason for our actions, there is some deep sense that it ought not to be this way. We ought to act in a different manner and be better at coping. Then, after weeks or months, if the feelings persist, we begin to think that maybe something is wrong with our mental state. Surely we should have begun to get a grip of ourselves by now? Not necessarily.

Although I never met him face to face, I was immensely impressed by a fifteen-year-old boy who phoned me one day. He had heard that I worked with bereaved people and wondered if I would go and see his mother. She had hardly stopped crying for a whole year. His father had committed suicide and she was totally devastated. It was not an easy decision but I explained that unless his mother came to see me under her own initiative, then it might not be of any real help to see her. He understood, but also explained to his mother how concerned he was for her. In response to that obvious and deep concern, the mother did make what was a very great effort and came to visit me. While RANI'S story was highly personal and unique to her, it has many strands that could be compared to other similar situations.

Expected to play second fiddle to a very domineering father, Rani's husband had been faced with running the family business, following his father's sudden collapse and death. The responsibility terrified him. Whereas previously he had never even been allowed to sign a cheque, now he found himself making decisions that affected the lives of around thirty workers. It was all too much for him. After three years and several attempts at suicide he was eventually successful in killing himself.

Initially, Rani's GP had prescribed sleeping pills but he had sensibly refused to give her further medication. He had reassured Rani that she was neither going mad nor in need of tranquillizers. Her suffering was tied up with her feelings of grief.

It was a blessing that Rani's doctor had not turned her grief into

an illness. He had provided reassurance and had encouraged her
to stick with the feelings she was experiencing.

At our first meeting I realized that Rani badly needed to talk
about her husband. At the end of the meeting I suggested that
she bring along some photographs of him to our second meeting
and she agreed. As we looked at those photographs, Rani continued to speak of her love for him – as she had done in the first
session. She looked at their wedding photographs, the photographs of their three children as babies, and then when they
were growing up; she talked about holidays and anniversaries.
But as she talked she began to get angry and then burst out with
tremendous rage, 'The bloody fool, throwing all this away. The
bastard, leaving me to carry the business and the family. The
selfish, stupid, weak, bastard. How could he have done this to
me?' Rani sat and wept but the weeping seemed to have a
different quality to it. It was no longer choked and fought back,
tears were flooding down her cheeks.

There was no doubt about her love for her husband and the
happiness that as a family they had shared. In her culture it
would have been hard enough to get really angry with a partner
in the flesh; it was so much more difficult when he was gone
for ever. If that was not enough, mixed with the guilt that she
had been unable to prevent the tragedy, Rani was hurt that her
husband had left her with all his responsibilities. But if she raged
at him in his absence, she faced the possibility that everything
about him would be lost – all the good times and all the happy
memories as well. However, harbouring that anger had resulted
in depression and perpetual tears. Letting go of it involved taking
an enormous risk, but once this was taken Rani never looked
back.

We had originally agreed to meet for six sessions. At the end
of the fourth session Rani said, 'I realise that we had thought it
might be necessary to meet several more times. I will of course
stick to that if you wish but, to be honest, I would be coming
for your sake rather than my own. I really did feel I was going
insane. Now I know it wasn't that at all – it was the pent-up
madness of rage.' I have to admit that I still had my doubts and
thought it might be better if Rani visited a few more times but,

since she appeared certain, it seemed important to trust her judgement.

Things do not always work out as they did for Rani, but she proved to be absolutely right. Had she visited me any longer it would have been to calm my own anxieties rather than to meet any need which she had. I never saw Rani again but, two years later, I did hear that she had taken the family business by the scruff of the neck, and that it was thriving – no mean feat for an Asian woman with no previous business experience and a staff mostly of men.

The doctor in Rani's story helped by not succumbing to her request for medication to deaden the pain. It must often be a very difficult tightrope to tread, since for very many patients medication is a definite lifeline. I am not alone, however, in believing that listening and talking therapies are very much to be preferred in the vast majority of situations. Are pills so often prescribed because they are easier and quicker? One young man, admitted into the psychiatric ward of a mental hospital for the third time in a matter of months, put it quite clearly:

> My girlfriend was killed in a street accident. We had a row, she packed her case, walked out on me, straight under a bus. As if filling me with pills is going to make any difference! I feel guilty as hell; no amount of pills can ever change that. Why won't the doctors listen?

GRIEF, FAITH AND GUILT

You do not have to be a theologian or a saint to register the fact that faith provides very many people with enormous encouragement and hope in their times of loss. But sometimes religion can get in the way and actually prevent people from grieving in a way that could be beneficial for them.

I have met many people like Dorothy, whose story was featured in chapter 1. Her elderly mother had died and it seemed cruel and hurtful to her. She had come to question whether it was still possible to talk of a loving God. For other people, it is not just the question of suffering that poses a problem. I suspect that many religious people are afraid to grieve, to get angry with God, to feel all those different feelings because it also makes them feel guilty. After all, isn't this an affront – the fact that any old body is putting God in the dock? The end result is perfectly simple. Since you cannot voice doubts and frustrations, and if you cannot 'simply believe', then you must have lost your faith. One possible alternative – a passive, unquestioning belief – is sometimes just a convenient blanket, covering up all those uncomfortable doubts and unvoicable questions.

At other times faith is used as a barricade – to repel those feelings. In chapter 2 we saw how Denise and Martin had moved to the country where they bought a shop with their savings. Denise had fallen seriously ill and all their carefully laid plans had to be changed. In the event, the couple turned to religion. A priest assured Denise that she need never fear because God's healing hand would be held out to her, as long as she truly believed. Ignoring the diagnosis of her condition as chronic and irreversible, she signed up for Lourdes. The shop was sold to finance these trips. So far she has made three visits with no change to her condition. Some may argue that such trips have enabled Denise to keep hoping. On the other hand it might be thought that these excursions offer only a cruel mirage. Are they really a reassuring support or are they a mechanism for the denial of a life-sized problem?

At this point I admit to my own experiences and strong feelings in this particular area. My first child was born prematurely and died while we were in Taiwan. The feelings of grief and distress were intense. I will always be grateful for the genuine kindness that we received from our Canadian and American missionary colleagues. However, the remnants of anger still remain from some of the letters of 'comfort' that we received. Not only were there the generally well-meant, but for all that, unhelpful comments, such as 'You will soon be able to have another child' or 'There must have been something dreadfully wrong with the baby' or 'If it had lived it might have been disabled'; there were also accusing and angry comments: 'The Bible says . . . so why don't you accept it?' and 'You are missionaries, you are letting God down by saying . . .' or 'As a priest you should be setting a better example.' The mixture of guilt and hurt took a very long time to get over. Yet, coming to terms with that powerful mixture of feelings contributed to decisions taken later, on the direction of my future working and personal life.

Some years after my first daughter's death, while working as a group therapist, I was attending a group for patients in a Scottish psychiatric hospital. One patient was speaking about her own grief and how her Kirk faith seemed to be standing between her and her ability to release her emotions. I started to say:

> Do you think it's a mistake to allow the Kirk faith, the Bible or religion to deny how real and important your feelings are? It sounds as though you are having to choose between respect for your own feelings and respect for what the Kirk teaches.

As I started to say this I began to cry. I was not just crying – but weeping from the very depths inside me. I was as embarrassed as hell and felt very foolish, but I could do absolutely nothing about it. It was then that I came to understand the destructive power of guilt and shame. It was not just those well-intentioned – and not so well-intentioned – letters that had caused me to barricade my feelings up inside. There was obviously within me an answering response to those accusations. I also felt I was letting everyone down, and that if I really believed the Bible words 'all things work together for good, to those who believe . . .' then I should be totally accepting of the loss and hopeful for the future.

Another lesson was that therapist, nurse, clergyman and doctor each share a common world of hurt and loss with my Scottish patient – and every other patient. However we label people to keep them separate from ourselves – doctor and patient, therapist and client, minister and member – we are no different in the way we feel the experiences of disillusionment or despair.

I had been faced, as had the Scottish lady, with an idealistic expectation that faith should meet all my needs. No matter the question, faith must be the 'jackpot' answer. For the mourner, however, to be whisked from shock to acceptance in one bound is unlikely to prove beneficial. There are for most of us too many thoughts remaining to be mulled over, too many feelings that still need to be experienced; there are just too many pieces of the jigsaw that need to be closely examined then reassembled before we can begin to feel a whole person once again.

WHAT ABOUT THE CHILDREN?

Can children cope with bad news? Must they be protected from it? Should we be more willing to share loss and sorrow with them? To a certain extent it's understandable to try to keep the 'unpleasant' side of life from youngsters, and it is certainly very difficult to know how to best inform children without alarming them unnecessarily. Don't take for granted, however, that children wouldn't want to, or shouldn't go to a funeral or a cremation. Why should they be denied the chance to say their 'goodbyes' when the rest of us have the opportunity?

Many adults bitterly regret the fact that, when they were young, their parents decided to conceal the news of a parental separation, or that they weren't told about some other major upset in the family when it was perfectly clear that something was going on. Sometimes it is a relief to know the facts, rather than go through the terror of imagining what might be happening. In the case of a marriage break-up, instead of being helped or protected, the children are left with a feeling of guilt because, underneath, they suspect they may have been responsible for it.

Andrea had agreed to take her eighteen-year-old nephew into her family. Rob had managed to get a job near where Andrea and her family lived and it seemed like an ideal arrangement. Rob usually returned to his own home at weekends. Andrea's own three children soon made great friends with Rob but in the case of her nine-year-old son STEVE it was more a matter of hero worship. Before long, Steve was supporting the same football team as Rob, was wearing the same type of clothing and watching the same television programmes.

Then, one morning, Rob failed to come down to breakfast

before setting off for work. At first Andrea called up the stairs to him, then after a while, she knocked on his bedroom door and went in. Andrea found Rob had taken an overdose and was already dead. Following the initial shock, one of Andrea's first thoughts was for Steve. How on earth was she going to tell him?

That night Andrea and her husband sat the children down and explained, without going into detail, that Rob had died. The family weren't religious but, none the less, they decided that it might soften the blow for Steve if they added 'He has gone to be with Jesus'. For some children this may have been a help but for Steve it proved a mistake. From then onwards he talked constantly of wanting to go to Jesus – so that he could be with Rob as well. Problems can arise with other euphemisms that are used in place of that tricky word, 'death'. For example, it has been found that if a child's death is explained away as 'going to sleep', the surviving children in the family have been frightened to go to bed at night.

All too often we as parents are highlighting our own fears and discomforts when we try to avoid the challenge of explaining the facts. The confusion about death can be our own and it is ourselves, and not the children, who are in need of protection. It is not unusual for parents who have had a stillborn child, or a child who has died in hospital, to immediately say, 'My other children were so looking forward to having a baby sister. How can I go home without one?'

The decision to tell a child the truth takes on a whole new dimension when 'the truth' has specific implications for that child's health and well-being. No one would pretend that the task of explaining to a child that a leg or an arm needs to be amputated is ever going to be anything less than appallingly difficult. There is little wonder that parents decide that their child should not be told of its impending death. But you can't help but wonder if it might actually be helpful if young children were told certain facts about their future.

Take the case of someone like JIMMY, a five-year-old with terminal cancer. Although he obviously knew he was very poorly, Jimmy was not aware of the severity of his illness and was terribly afraid and angry. He became the scourge of his children's ward:

at one moment refusing to communicate with anyone, at the next hurling abuse in a rich mixture of curses. His parents were adamant that nothing should be said to him about his condition. For the father, especially, this abrasive behaviour suggested that his son was fighting for survival. When the boy at last became more amenable the father was angry with the nurses, as he saw this as the beginning of the end for his son.

On another children's ward a terminally ill nine-year-old said to the nurses, 'I know Mummy has been crying outside but it would be easier if she cried with me. I want to cry as well but I can't because it might upset her more.' When the mother was told of this, her reaction was to share her sorrow with her son and she was able to take a much greater part in caring for him. For many parents, the chance to help make a child's bed or share in simple bathing and nursing routines removes the feelings of helplessness which can add to the burden of sorrow.

Recently a young French primary school teacher achieved 'national hero' status when she protected her class of children from a threatened suicide bombing. One parent was interviewed after the gunman had been shot dead and all the children had been released. Her major concern, the parent admitted, was how she should answer the question from her four-year-old daughter, 'What happened to the man?' She had already decided that she was going to tell her the truth.

Childhood is full of losses in the normal course of events. Loss is all part and parcel of growing up. Disappointments in early friendships, the death of a loved pet, the heartbreak of a first broken romance, the loss of a parent – all are likely to be more devastating for a youngster than for an adult. It is very likely that some childhood 'naughtiness' results from the struggle to cope with the feelings aroused by loss. It is hard enough for a child to explain physical pain so, where fearful emotions are involved, these may be converted into fantastical terrors of serpents and ghosts as well as unacceptable behaviour.

Gradually the myths that have surrounded physical pain in children are being cleared away. Like the suggestion that children do not feel pain as much as adults – in fact, tolerance to pain increases with age. Another myth is that an active child must not be feeling pain. Increased activity may actually be a sign of pain and playing may be used by the child as a diversion, to help cope with it. Other fables concerning emotional distress describe children's obliviousness to anything which badly needs to be cleared away. Many a schoolteacher will, however, point to the deterioration in a child's behaviour and learning performance when his or her parents are breaking up.

Family grieving which is shared more openly and honestly with children could be a preparation for later life. How often have you heard someone say that what they valued most highly in their upbringing was the fact they could 'really talk' with their parents? Discussing a loss and giving the child an opportunity to air his or her feelings will go a long way to reducing the hurt when grief is encountered.

SENDING OUT SIGNALS

It is sometimes hard to know how to react to the grief of others. The best thing we can do is listen for signals. It should soon become clear whether people wish to talk or not. Either way, when we learn of someone else's bereavement the simplest first step is just to say we are sorry to hear about it. Many people exclaim: 'I knew that J's marriage had broken up/child had died/ wife had left home, and I just didn't know what to say . . .' The point is, we don't even have to say anything. Sending a card with a printed message then signing it will indicate to the bereaved person that we are thinking of them.

MARY likes to talk about her husband who died a few years ago. She still badly feels the pain of loss but she brings his name into the conversation, quite naturally, when the opportunity arises: 'Jeremy and I often used to drive to Italy . . .' or 'This was one of Jeremy's books; he was a great fan of . . .' Mary is showing that she is relaxed and willing to talk about her husband and it is therefore all right for her listener to refer to him.

Others make it quite clear how they want others to react – or not react. I remember hearing about a former colleague whose baby had died two days after birth. She relayed a message to her office that, on her return to work, she did not want to discuss her loss. When a few weeks later she did return it was, on the surface at least, 'business as usual' and, as far as I know, she never did refer to her child's death.

HOW TO COPE WITH SOMEONE ELSE'S LOSS

People who have recently suffered a loss often say that one of the worst things to bear is the fact other people appear so uncomfortable with them. They talk of acquaintances crossing the road rather than having to speak, of former friends who suddenly stop inviting them round. Here are some ways with which to deal with another person's loss:

- Don't worry about saying 'the wrong thing'. If nothing else, simply say 'I am sorry to hear about . . .' and leave it at that, without expecting a reply. Even if the bereaved person doesn't reply, they will probably be thankful for the fact that you acknowledged their loss.
- If you find it hard to voice your thoughts, just send a card. It may already have a printed message inside and you will only have to sign it. Again, what may appear inadequate to you is likely to be appreciated.
- Listen. Once you have offered your condolences, let the bereaved person talk. They may be quiet for weeks, then suddenly start to speak about their loss. Enable them to do this. Don't feel you have to fill the quiet spaces in between. They will find words in their own time and 'filling up' the gaps will only hinder this process.
- Resist the temptation to relate your own experiences. The person bearing the loss will be immersed in their own thoughts and, in the initial stages, is unlikely to reap comfort from hearing about someone else's troubles.
- If the person bearing the loss – be it death, marriage break-up, job loss or whatever – starts to cry, then let them. Try not to worry about your own reactions, like thinking about what to say, just let them cry and give them a tissue. Try to find them a quiet place to be upset in.
- If you want to write a letter to a bereaved person, it is not

always necessary to be sombre and formal. If you personally knew the one who has died, you could write about the good times you enjoyed together. Those who have lost elderly parents have spoken of letters received from their parent's friends, relating incidents from their youth. They have found great comfort in being reminded about how their parent was when they were alive and enjoying life.

- Don't always assume that the bereaved person will not want to be reminded of their loss. Sometimes they will want and need to reflect on it.

CHAPTER 5

Coping With Grief

There is a great deal to be learned from all experiences of loss. I am constantly grateful for a part of my childhood, spent sitting round a winter fireside just talking about the past. It was in the days before every home had a television and, as we were one of the last families in our street to have a TV, there was less to distract us from thinking and talking together. My grandmother, who lived with us, told us all about life at the turn of the century and into the 1920s. My mother painted a colourful picture of the 1930s and 40s. It was mostly talk about people and it was quite possible that I knew more about my school friends' and neighbours' family backgrounds than they did themselves. Of course, not all the memories were happy ones and there were many discussions about what had happened, what had gone wrong and how things might have been different had other decisions been taken. But there was nothing negative or regretful about all of this. Instead, there was a genuine interest in weighing up and understanding the past. There was also a real desire to learn from it and to try to do things differently in the future.

I am personally convinced of the value of looking back to see how we, ourselves, have used our own personal resources to cope in the past. Add this to finding out how others have managed in their loss experiences and accepting practical advice, and we can achieve some kind of balance between positive and negative reactions to loss, stress and change.

The personal stories included in this book illustrate that there are as many different reactions to loss as there are types of loss. Each experience – be it death, divorce, unemployment, amputation or stillbirth – is unique in its own way. Take death, for example. Each death is different – not just because of the situation involved but because it may be sudden and completely unexpected, predictable and very quick, or long and drawn out. Death comes in the womb before birth, at the end of old age and at every stage in between. It happens through illness, accidents, murder, suicide, natural causes and in war situations. Each person involved brings his or her own past experiences and personal history into the equation; maybe there was a happy or sad childhood, a fulfilled or empty marriage, an extended family or no relationships at all, a satisfied or discontented working life. All these factors influence the way loss is accepted – or denied. It may be rejected, buried, or masked through drinking or drug-taking or by blaming others or ourselves.

Whatever the circumstances, there are a variety of ways which may help us inch along the grieving process to those first stages of recovery. Simple information is invaluable for helping people get a better bearing on their situation; keeping some continuity after loss can help stabilize; exercising a certain amount of control over your own situation can provide a stepping-stone onto firmer ground; outside support in the form of self-help groups provides more information and the chance to exchange experiences; understanding and knowing yourself better can focus and clarify emotions and feelings.

IN POSSESSION OF THE FACTS

Lack of basic and essential information surrounding a loss can lead to even greater trauma when grieving. Confusion around her husband's terminal illness – how much he knew and how much she should discuss with him – created many uncertainties for MARY. Mary had been married to Jeremy, her second husband, for only a few years when it was discovered he was terminally ill with a tumour on the brain. Mary says that the greatest difficulties arose through not knowing how much he understood about the implications of his illness – and whether he knew it was terminal. Mary explains:

> We had travelled a long way to see the consultant who, after first seeing my husband, came down to the waiting room, stood in the doorway, and gave me the news. I was told he would have a year – possibly more – to live. I asked the doctor whether Jeremy knew. He explained my husband had been told that he was seriously ill. But although my husband knew he had a tumour he seemed confident that he would become well again.

Over the next few months Jeremy appeared to recover some of his former health but then began to get ill once more. He eventually underwent pioneering surgery, but sadly it had come too late and was not successful. However, Jeremy continued to appear to believe he was going to recover. This caused many uncertainties for Mary, who didn't know how much she should discuss with him. Perhaps he was trying to remain optimistic in order to protect her. Because the operation had taken place some distance from the couple's home, there was no real opportunity to meet with the experts and clarify exactly how much Jeremy knew of his illness – and how much it would be wise to discuss with him. Mary became more confused and deeply worried about just how frank she could be.

Their own GP provided neither additional information nor further guidance or suggestions for support. Mary sensed it was as though he did not feel comfortable with the idea of death; he seemed to be out of his depth with this dying patient. This is not as unusual as you might suppose among health care workers. While many are undoubtedly greatly skilled and sensitive in dealing with loss and grief situations, there are those who, having been taught to cure and save lives, simply can't handle death, which they perceive as failure. So the GP never once visited Mary or Jeremy at home. Mary says:

> There was no chance for me to talk to an outside counsellor or to experts who could advise me. I had no idea that there were such things as Macmillan nurses who could help me. Maybe they could have spoken with my husband and found out how much he knew – whether he was trying to protect me from worry, or whether he actually wanted and needed to talk to me about his illness. As it was I just couldn't be sure whether Jeremy, who was an intelligent man, knew if he was dying or not.

Mary and Jeremy had always been so close and yet she didn't know whether to be honest with him towards the end.

Then everything changed. One day Mary spoke to a young locum GP who was standing in for their usual doctor. He very swiftly realized that Mary was in great need of support and put her in touch with a Macmillan nurse and a bereavement counsellor with experience of the terminally ill and their carers. Suddenly, only a few weeks before her husband's death, Mary had the chance to voice her fears and worries and get practical help in making decisions about how to deal with them. The bereavement counsellor made a suggestion for which Mary will be forever grateful, and one that she simply wouldn't have thought of – that she make a tape of herself and Jeremy talking, to keep for the future. The nurse suggested ways that Mary might try to discover exactly how much Jeremy knew of his illness through their usual conversation. Unfortunately by this time he was very confused and it was also hard to understand what he was saying.

Several years on, Mary has made a new life but still feels great regret at the lack of information and ensuing uncertainty around her husband's illness. Because the support she and her husband received just before he died was of enormous help, she wishes she could have been put in touch with it earlier. She continues to mourn her loss. 'I still have some way to go and I feel much of this is due to my confusion in those first months, when my husband's condition was first diagnosed,' she says.

Being in possession of information and facts surrounding loss can help people build some kind of structure from which to cope with both the loss and the ensuing grief. Those who have experienced miscarriages and stillbirths have expressed the need to see some evidence of their dead children. However short a term that life has been, the child will have been felt in the womb; it will have kicked and moved; it will have been longed for, planned and prepared for. To the parents, that child will remain a real and deeply missed person in their lives.

Having a memento of the infant's birth as well as very comprehensive information about the circumstances of its death can assist the grieving process along its path. For the life of the infant to pass by unmarked is to intensify the sense of what has never been, but so nearly was. Even a small memorial card can register the fact of his or her brief presence in and passage through this world. Parents explain that this helps them accept the fact of their child's death and adjust to the reality of the loss. In addition to this, some kind of annual marking of the birth has helped parents considerably. A Service of Remembrance can be arranged in the hospital chapel and the infant's name inserted in the Book of Remembrance. Wherever it is possible and welcomed, a photograph of the infant will have been taken and presented to the family. All these simple rites of remembrance for children who have died before or after birth are a source of comfort to a great many parents.

ALAN, who was a nurse, and his wife SUSAN were full of praise for the treatment they received in a hospital baby unit. Without earlier warning of any possible difficulties, Susan was rushed into the baby unit where her daughter was born three weeks prematurely. She and Alan were told that Julie Ann was very poorly and was unlikely to survive. The couple were not regular church-attenders, although they had been married in church and their two-year-old son had been baptized. Susan's parents, sister and a very close friend were with her and, together with Alan, Susan decided to ask the hospital chaplain to baptize their baby.

The quite brief and simple service to baptize Julie Ann was

punctuated with floods of tears from each one of them. It had all come so suddenly. Twenty-four hours previously, everyone had been excited and expectant; now all hopes had been dashed. Some of the ward staff stayed for the service and openly shed tears for Alan, in particular, whom they knew and worked with. The couple received a baptism card from the chaplain and were told about the Book of Remembrance kept in the chapel.

Alan and his mother-in-law stayed with the infant until the last moments of her life. Susan was still very weak and needed treatment and rest, but when Alan came back to see her she knew that Julie Ann had died. They held each other and wept, and then joined the family in a small private room where the tiny, perfectly-formed baby was brought in and given to Susan to hold. It had not been possible to hold her earlier, when she had been in an incubator, with tubes attached to her small body. To each, being able to cuddle the person who had become a very important part of their lives and would always remain so, was of immense importance to them. They accepted a nurse's offer to use a Polaroid camera to take photographs. Alan and Susan were given time, understanding and made to feel as though nothing else mattered in the hospital at that moment. Their needs were of central importance and would be met.

Thinking afterwards about the level of care they all received, Alan and Susan said that, despite the painfulness of the experience, they felt safe and secure in the hands of the staff. They knew everything that could be done for Julie Ann had been done. They were in no doubt about the care of their own families for them but were really affected by the genuine feelings shown by the hospital staff. Despite the numbing shock of it all, they felt held and supported in a way they had found totally unexpected.

The funeral was a sad affair but, in its own way, it drew those unhappy events to a close. In many respects it was simply a great relief to get everything over. The couple were by then quite drained of all emotion. However, some months later they were presented with the opportunity to remember and reflect on all that happened at a memorial service. Having accepted the offer of an entry in the hospital Children's Book of Remembrance for Julie Ann, Alan and Susan received from the chaplain an invitation to the local church for the Annual Children's Service of Remembrance. Many other bereaved parents, as well as hospital staff members, were present. The simple service was moving, the talking among themselves over coffee afterwards was a comfort and an encouragement. During those months Alan and Susan had not spoken very much about all that happened and the event provided the chance to share what it had meant to them both.

In another sad story involving a child, a man described the value of the information he received very soon after his young son had died. He explained that he and his wife had felt completely paralysed after the event and were enormously grateful for counselling, which offered advice on what to expect – such as the physical symptoms of grief. At the time, because so much happened so quickly, information regarding funeral arrangements and the chance to discuss them and other practical issues with a counsellor was welcomed by him and his family.

Women have described their feelings of loss and helplessness when surgical procedures have not been explained, or when they haven't known the sex of their dead infant after the removal of a foetus. Male partners have related their anguish – often leading to unresolved grief – when they have been excluded from counselling regarding pregnancy terminations or other surgical procedures involving their partners. And it is not just the bereaved relative who appreciates the sharing of information. Nursing and other staff in hospitals have described their feelings of devastation when a patient they have known, or personally attended to, has died in their absence. They have related how no explanation of the death has been offered to hospital staff who have cared for the deceased and how, because they felt they were expected to 'take it all in their stride', they have continued to feel the loss. Some are even warned against crying at work, although thankfully this is becoming less common.

The increasingly human and compassionate contact between patient and medical practitioner is demonstrated in one hospital unit which treats cancer patients. Recognizing that patients are sometimes so anxious and frightened that they fail to take in the information that is being given to them regarding surgical treatments, such a mastectomy, the consultant records the interview, then gives the tape recording to the patient to take home and listen to again. This seems such a simple and practical idea it is surprising it is not more widely used.

It is just possible that Mary received other important information about Jeremy's treatment from her consultant but was too shocked to take it in at the time. This, together with the growing North American practice of making claims for malpractice in healthcare situations, could mean that the whole issue of how information is communicated needs even more careful examination. Examples of positive and helpful practice, like that of the taped interview, should certainly be extended.

Because of the stigma and the shame experienced by those who have suffered loss through a violent assault on their bodies, the majority of rapes go unreported. It was a brave decision that an elderly woman took when she agreed to release her name to the press and to be interviewed about her rape ordeal. Talking about that decision she explained that her initial reason had been to help catch the rapist. Then she realized her own experience could be useful to others, and she actually saw no reason she should feel ashamed for something which she could not have prevented. Talking about the incident became, in its own way, a part of the healing process.

This woman, in her late sixties, said that she believed a younger woman without her experience would not have coped so well. She had lost both her first and second husbands through illness and these events, she said, had helped to strengthen her. Previous losses had, for her, proved strengthening; they had served as a reservoir of experience upon which she could draw. Obviously that experience had convinced her that truthful information, both given and received, is a positive and powerful influence.

In other violent situations, such as murder, relatives of victims sometimes seek comfort in visiting the scene of the crime. They explain that, however upsetting the experience might be, they prefer to know the truth rather be haunted by their imaginations. Knowing the truth, being in possession of the full facts, understanding the circumstances surrounding a tragedy, can play a key role in the healing process. But again it is vitally important to stress that this is by no means the case for everyone, and that individuals need an element of choice and control over the information they are given.

Some cultures certainly do not welcome openness. Take the Japanese, for example, who place great value on lack of directness in all forms of everyday communication. Emotions are covered, dealings with each other and also with foreigners are woven into a distinctly complex structure of graded relationships. In a recent survey, when asked if they would like their doctor to let them know if they had cancer, 25 per cent replied that they wouldn't. Nearly 60 per cent said that they would not tell a relative who was suffering from cancer. Public figures disappear and then reappear without explanation, despite their evident ill-health.

CONTINUITY COUNTS

For many people, retirement can mean a complete change in lifestyle and one they are ill-prepared for. While some relish the chance to spend 'real' time pursuing the interests they never had time for when working, others suddenly find that they had no interests outside work and life is overwhelmingly different. Recognizing the potential impact of retirement on employees, enlightened companies today run retirement seminars. Several months before they actually leave the company, those who are coming up for retirement are invited to attend in order to find out more about subjects such as finance, use of time, the likely effect on a partnership in the home, how to keep healthy, and exploration of hobbies and interests. All of this may sound a simple matter of common sense but the effect of those changes in apparently trivial ways can cause tremendous conflicts.

DORIS had actually passed her retirement age but had eased into semi-retirement through a part-time cleaning job. Each day she would get her husband's breakfast, make his sandwiches for lunch and get him off to work. By seven-thirty she was at her own office and had everything ready for the nine o'clock arrival of the staff. She finished at ten-thirty and was back at home and had tidied the house by lunch time. Most afternoons she had a whole range of activities to fully occupy her.

Then her husband retired. He stayed in bed later and when she returned from work was either still in bed or was just having breakfast. He didn't seem to know what to do with his day. Suddenly, her well-organized and entirely satisfying life was totally overturned. While, to begin with, Doris was glad for her husband, that he had reached his retirement after a very hard-working life, she began to resent his intrusion and eventually became very depressed. His gain was her loss. Neither Doris nor her husband had any idea what full retirement might mean in practice so they had not thought to prepare for the changes that it brought.

There are few benefits to be found in the widespread recession of the 1990s, but perhaps one positive aspect is a greater understanding of the implications of redundancy. This won't make it any easier to be unemployed but, with every section of society being affected, initial stigmas have been reduced, losses incurred are more openly discussed and there are greater attempts to offer practical assistance as well as emotional support.

BEWARE OF SWEEPING CHANGE

Beware of making quick, rash decisions after loss. Sweeping changes may well prove a good idea in the long run but, if taken too soon, they can prove an additional burden.

When ELSA'S marriage broke up she began to feel angry and completely dissatisfied with her entire life. After only a few months she decided to leave her well-paid, secure and glamorous job and set up her own business. 'I had become tired of what I perceived as a superficial working life dealing with meaningless everyday problems. I wanted to do something more useful,' she explains. So Elsa set up business on her own, seeking to explore areas of work which she considered to be 'more worthwhile'. Apart from the fact she now had a large mortgage and household running expenses to pay on her own, her income was greatly reduced and work was thin on the ground. In the end she found herself accepting all kinds of jobs in order to meet her bills.

This, of course, added a further burden to that of the loss of her marriage relationship. Although Elsa eventually managed to make her business work, it was a long and hard struggle. Looking back, she believes it would have made life a whole lot easier if she had stayed put for at least another year.

> Maybe if someone had sat me down and spelled out the implications of what I was doing, I might have listened. But subtle asides and tentative 'Are you sure you know what you are doing?' type questions were wasted on me. I know only too well that pure 'advice' is usually a waste of time. But I do think that friends could be less afraid of speaking out honestly. When bad things happen, you just can't think clearly. No-punches-pulled, straight talking has its place.

When a partner dies, sometimes the remaining partner tells how they find some comfort in continuing simple household routines that were once organized together. Adults who have lived with an elderly parent in a large family home all their lives often choose to remain there alone. Rather than move somewhere smaller, they decide to preserve their memories in the family home. Bereaved relatives often keep all the possessions of their deceased loved ones – sometimes for years. At times this is commented on as a possible means of denying the loss. Others may encourage the bereaved to 'do some good' by giving their loved one's clothes and belongings to a charitable cause. Behind this encouragement is the suggestion that holding on to belongings is a bad thing and that 'clinging to the past' is questionable. Illustrating how different our responses to loss can be, SEAN looks back on his reactions following the death of his wife after a very long period of illness:

> She died in this room where we are talking. Within hours of her death I had taken her bed back upstairs. By the next morning I decided that this room would be the first one I'd redecorate. Within twenty-four hours I had the walls stripped for painting. [Two weeks after his wife's death, Sean had disposed of her belongings.] After three weeks I was

back at work and carrying on with all my usual pursuits. I felt that "life must go on" and I was rather proud of the way I was coping.

I managed to keep this up for almost two years and then I broke down. I became very sad and depressed and, far from coping, I could see that I had done an excellent job of denying all that her death and the loss of her presence had actually meant to me. I remember meeting a man whose wife had been in the Salvation Army. Years after her death he not only had kept her uniform but he brushed it every week. I was at the other end of that scale. Three years on, I now feel more confident that I have coped. I also feel a lot stronger and a more fulfilled person because I have let grief take its course.

A classic time to make a complete break with the past is retirement. It often leads to people selling their homes and moving to completely different areas, such as the countryside or the coast. Not only do they have to get used to an unfamiliar district and make a new circle of acquaintances but, if they only visited in the summer, then they may not have considered the personal discomforts a tough countryside winter can bring.

For people who have thoroughly researched their move it has led to a new and stimulating period of their lives. For others – like the couple I once met on a train – it turns out a disaster. With great excitement they had sold up and invested in a boarding house near Blackpool. After just one winter it had proved too cold and bleak for them, so they sold up once more and returned to their previous home area. With hindsight, they felt they should have given themselves time to work out what retirement was all about before taking a giant step away from their roots.

Change is inevitable and has to be accommodated in all our lives. But sometimes – particularly in the case of grief following loss – some continuity can prove stabilizing.

A DEGREE OF CONTROL

Loss and grief can knock us totally off balance. Getting information and keeping some things the same are ways to recover some kind of control. Where very sick children are concerned, a parent can find great comfort in being able to play some part in the hospital routine of caring for their child. Terminally ill people who are aware of their circumstances decide to write wills, organize financial arrangements and make funeral plans for themselves, where they carefully select the music and readings. Even if they have no control over the disease that has afflicted them, they can still manage their affairs in preparation for death. In a whole range of circumstances, self-help groups are designed to enable a degree of control to return to the lives of people who have found that circumstances have overtaken them.

Associated closely with personal control is the whole issue of independence. One of the biggest losses faced by so many people as they combat the mounting pressures of old age is loss of independence. Once again, all the responses common to grief rear up. Anger, guilt and depression are everyday feelings in the emotional lives of the elderly. Even more fundamental is the element of denial.

EDGAR was labelled as the 'difficult' patient of the ward. Although he regularly took communion from me and was always appreciative of this ministry to him, I was privately informed that in between such visits his language usually verged on the explicitly blue rather than the more saintly purple. From the very first time we met, Edgar made it abundantly clear that hospital and the residential home that was to follow, were not for him. Edgar had been a widower for fifteen years and now, in his late eighties, he had every intention of returning home as soon as his broken hip had healed.

'You can tell them from me, vicar,' he would say, 'if they expect me to give up my home, then they have another think coming! I can cook, I still bake my own bread and make jam. I would not be able to do any of that in one of those places for old people.' The trouble was, Edgar's own house had lots of stairs and this was not the first time he had fallen down. There were genuine fears for his safety and, while no one wanted to impose a solution on him, there were professional obligations that needed to be taken seriously. All of this was mumbo jumbo to Edgar. Despite complications that eventually kept him in hospital for six months, not a day went by without him reminding anyone within earshot that 'Nobody can stop me going to my own home.'

Despite days of depression, regular bouts of anger and aggressive lack of co-operation, he never gave up the struggle to retain control over his own future. 'Take away my independence, and I might as well be dead,' was his theme tune. To everyone's astonishment, his fight against the voices of reason was eventually successful. Two years on he continues very contentedly to manage his own life, with the help that he chooses to accept, in his own home.

If only every such situation involving elderly people was resolved so satisfactorily. The 'Care in the Community' initiative, launched in April 1993, aims to provide the necessary back-up for elderly people like Edgar. It means they can retain their personal dignity and a real measure of individual control over their lives. As with other initiatives – like the one that returns formerly hospitalized patients to a community setting – much will depend on the financial resources made available to the programme to show whether it is successful or not. Old age does not have to be a downward helter-skelter into a pit of depression. But the losses that are inevitably part and parcel of the ageing process require the right resources.

In an earlier chapter we saw the impact on patients and staff of the closure of one large psychiatric hospital, and its incorporation into a neighbouring hospital. Initial research into the effects of that move suggested that there was a greater likelihood of earlier death for some patients as a result of the upheaval. Some detrimental effects were unavoidable. However, other patients were the beneficiaries of a less maternalistic regime of care. There were many instances of patients who were placed in newly decorated wards and expected, with the appropriate encouragement, to take a greater responsibility for themselves. Their appearance and personalities developed very markedly. Whatever the physical, educational or emotional limitations that we human beings may be confronted with, we have a habit of surviving. But take away our right to make important personal decisions and we become incomplete as human beings.

It is not necessary to observe just the elderly or the incapacitated. How many people have come out of institutions, such as the Army, totally unprepared for civilian life? I am well aware that the Forces have changed radically since my National Service days, but I suspect that some of those experiences remain. I can still hear my sergeant-major bellowing at me, 'You're not paid to think!' Having to live in a regime of regulations, with your housing provided and career structures clearly mapped out, has certain advantages. But it can also leave the recipient of such structured living at a real disadvantage when faced with the unpredictable demands of civilian life. Whether that structure is the Forces, prison or long-term incarceration in a hospital, losing the right to make personal choices, and therefore control of your own life, is ultimately damaging.

In the same way, placing the responsibility for choices that are central to our future lives into the hands of another person – be that person human or divine – can be less of an altruistic act of faith than putting our trust in another. All of us, at certain points in our lives, need encouragement, support, straight talking and constructive criticism. However, the moment we off-load responsibility onto others for decisions that we should make for ourselves then we are giving up far more than we realize.

Looked at from another perspective, it is possible that we are denying that our childhood has been lost. That child, tucked away somewhere in all of us, longs for the time when it was possible to feel safe and secure. If we failed to enjoy the benefits of loving parents, our hearts long even more for the time that never was. Rather like Sarah, in chapter 1, far removed from the security of her city friendships, she suddenly realized that her depression was not just the result of her present feelings of rural isolation. It was also linked to her lonely childhood. Maybe all those feelings associated with grief are embedded much deeper in our personalities than we would have suspected.

KNOW YOURSELF

You may have tried out the exercise in the first chapter which involved the simple process of drawing a straight line and making notches on it to indicate significant losses in your life. Try the same exercise again, with a slight variation, and then compare it with the earlier exercise.

Draw a straight line and this time the first step will be to make notches that mark significant stages in your life for example, starting school, leaving school/starting work or further education, getting married, birth of a first child, etc. Select your own particular life 'landmarks'. The next stage is to identify on the lifeline what your own significant losses have been and when they occurred in your life. Jot down what each of those losses were so you can refer back to them.

This very simple exercise offers a rich resource of stored experience on which you can draw, and from which there is a great deal to be learned. The pity of this personal experience is that instead of being stored in the pantry, where you can nip in and take out what you need, it tends to be hidden away in the deep freeze and is not so readily accessible. Now try something else:

Without thinking too much about it, draw a second line below the first one. Running your pen along the paper, draw upwards to signify the good times, and downwards for the not so good ones. It will, of course, be on the wavy side. Compare and contrast the earlier straight and now the wavy lifelines, asking yourself: when? where? what? how? See if they shed any light on the why? questions.

It is entirely up to you how far you want to go with this exercise. Do you want to ask yourself about the points which had particular significance in your life? Were they times of change and did they arouse very different feelings in you? How different were the feelings that were aroused in the different experiences? Are there attitudes or types of behaviour that have changed in your life as a result? Are there repeating patterns of reaction that you can spot? Is it possible to pick out where these patterns began?

Since this book has focused on loss, a vital series of questions might be asked – even if they may be both uncomfortable and possibly scary. On the first straight line you identified at which points your particular losses have taken place. These are likely to be at any point along the whole of your lifeline. Compare when your times of loss happened with the wavy line. How did you react to loss? How do you feel about your reactions – can you accept them? Which losses caused the greatest traumas?

There are other simple ways of putting our experiences into some kind of perspective. All of them are aimed at helping to see ourselves more clearly, to understand ourselves a little better and to enable us to live with more confidence in our ability to cope:

- Keep a diary in times of particular stress: observe what is happening to you. Alternatively, just write down, in as much detail as possible, all that is going through your mind at a particular point of time, during a period of great stress.
- Make a tape recording and speak out about all that is jumbled up and rumbling around in your thoughts; listen to yourself later and maybe share it with someone else and talk about it.
- Make a list of ten things which you most value in life, then jot down from your lifeline those things which have been lost. Ask yourself about the values, hopes and aspirations that remain.

There are all kinds of possible ways of responding to causes of grief in our lives. There are times when you need to run and hide; at other times it is appropriate to cry out and complain; we have seen people who have been thrown into confusion or have been icily cool in their need to make a definite decision; some people talk while others withdraw. All of these responses are natural and play their part in enabling the sufferer to cope.

However, to give ourselves the chance to fully adjust to a life that can never be the same as it was prior to the loss, we shall need to 'invest in ourselves'. These exercises are not the kind of examination which you have to pass. They offer an opportunity to cherish your own experience, to believe in the worth of what you have learned, and they are intended to underline the right you have to trust your own insights. It takes time to reflect and think about yourself, but you are worth it and you owe it to yourself. I am not pretending it is easy but do you really need to be afraid?

CHAPTER 6

Moving On

What happens when you begin to move out of the initial stages of grief? How do you cope with your loss? Do you get up and 'get over' it? Do you ever really 'recover'? Is there a grieving time span to be expected? Needless to say, everyone copes differently.

The length of time in mourning will depend largely on the individual. Some people elect to set goals for themselves because it's the way they are and the way they have always worked. They feel more secure working within a structure, so they sit down and rationally work out a plan of action for the future. Others take a less pragmatic attitude, preferring to let events take their course. They say, 'You just don't know what life has in store so you may as well live for the moment.' Rather than plot a route, they drift along, recognizing small signposts to recovery here and there. Then there are those who appear to remain in their grief, prompting others to pose that tired old chestnut, 'Isn't it about time you "got over" it all?' Particularly interesting are the many people who, when asked how they have coped, reply that they weren't even aware that they had coped at all. Yet, they give every appearance to onlookers that they have a measured and optimistic view of life.

While there are the various components of grief – shock, denial, anger, guilt and usually a degree of acceptance – each person's loss is unique and individual in a whole host of ways. Adjusting to a new set of circumstances and re-creating life after grief is no less personal and brimming with variety. In previous chapters we have seen evidence of the courage and vitality that is discovered by those who have had the most debilitating experiences of loss. The phrase that is repeated again and again is: 'I would not have thought it was possible.' Time and time again there are examples of understatement and genuine modesty about what has been achieved. People say: 'I did what I thought was right', or 'I just tried to do the best I could', when they have invested immense energy and sheer, gritty determination in trying to create a quality of life after grief.

While there will usually be many mixed emotions involved in a loss, not all of these are negative. In chapter 5 we heard the story of Mary and Jeremy. The lack of information surrounding Jeremy's terminal illness had created great confusion and added to the trauma for Mary. Before she married Jeremy, Mary had been married to her first husband for twenty years. Her eventual divorce came as an enormous relief. She had been through many unhappy years in this relationship, ten of which she had remained in for the sake of the children. Now, thankfully, it was all over and her long-term relationship with Jeremy could at last be allowed to flourish. It was what they had both hoped for over the past decade. The next five years were the happiest years of both their lives. The sixth was overshadowed by the news of Jeremy's terminal illness, leading to his death.

A year earlier, doctor's had warned Mary about Jeremy's illness. Even so, the initial shock and disbelief following his death had been no less intense. There was self-doubt and questioning; Mary repeatedly asked herself, 'Were we being punished for broken marriage vows?' Later, after Jeremy had died, Mary continued to wonder how much Jeremy had known about his terminal illness. Should she have discussed it with him more directly? Then there were doubts concerning her future on her own. 'I was still young. How could I survive without the best friend I have ever had or could have ever wished for?' Mary also harboured the fear of being perceived as a 'widow' and not an individual in her own right.

All these questions and worries were, to some extent, put on hold when Mary's elderly mother was taken ill and needed support for the next twelve months. Her mother's funeral – which actually took place at the same crematorium, with the same service, organized by the same undertakers, and attended by so many of the same friends – brought all those anxieties rushing back.

Now, looking back on her years of 'learning to cope', she still considers she has some way to travel to complete her journey of recovery. When Mary was asked what had helped her along the way, she offered the following significant points:

- Determination not to be bitter about what she had lost, but rather to feel thankful for all that was positive in her relationship with Jeremy.
- A resolve to 'not let things go'. Mary decided fairly early on that she would not stop looking after herself, that she would continue to take real care of her hair and clothes. Like many other people we have spoken to, she understood the importance of eating properly and learning to cook for one.
- A growing 'self-awareness', with the realization that her earlier unhappy marriage had left her with inner resilience and an ability to make tough decisions alone.
- Friends who both listened and talked – but above all respected her strengths; gratitude for the fact they recognized her ability to cope, which both reassured and encouraged her in the bad times.
- Mary 'scoured bookshelves for books that would help me to understand what was happening to me. Some I would throw across the room, when I tried to read them: they were not for me and didn't seem to know what they were talking about.' Others she thought had helped for a time but were no longer of use as she moved on. This was in its own way encouraging. It showed her that things were going in the right direction.
- Though she wishes she had done it while Jeremy was still well and lucid, Mary does have tapes of their conversations

and finds tremendous comfort in listening to his voice.
- Returning to her profession, though working only part-time: 'To be able to forget myself and think about what is going on all round me.'

Although Mary kept up her sporting and recreational activities – such as swimming, walking and tennis, which have all contributed to her new and entirely positive enjoyment of life – there are some activities which she enjoyed with Jeremy that she has no wish to continue, for the present at any rate. These include listening to his favourite composers, playing golf and dancing.

Mary has moved on – not just emotionally but geographically. However, in her new home she has both photographs of Jeremy and belongings that were very personal to him. She says she has created a new home for him as well, and suggests:

> This may be an element of denying his absence. I know he would have been very happy to have been with me in this house, and I think of him being here now. I would not rule out the possibility of meeting someone else but, for the moment, I treasure his presence with me in a very special way.

Mary feels she is going in the right direction. Imagination and hopes remain an important source of encouragement in thinking about Jeremy's presence with her but, as yet, dreams have not caught up. These are still stuck in the times of trauma around the marriage break-up. Mary is certain that the happier times will feature in her dreams at some future stage. It is, for her, one more indication that the healing journey has not yet reached its destination.

Fears still remain for Mary: 'that no one now really needs me'; that she may be lumped in with 'all the other widows'; or that friends could exclude her because she might be seen as a threat. There are other continuing questions that may have no tidy resolutions and which are ever-present in the back of her mind. She wonders whether her grief will ever be completely 'healed' or 'resolved' but this, she says, doesn't worry her. The major sense that she conveys is one of 'things going well and in the right direction'.

There is another interesting aspect to Mary's story. She has moved to a lovely new house, designed and planted a whole new garden, taken on part-time work, developed a circle of friends and a new life. She has accomplished all this in her new role as a 'single' woman. And yet, when asked how she has coped, she says, 'Well, I don't know that I do. I still get "troughs" of great sadness.' And yet it is clear to an onlooker that Mary is coping – and very successfully at that.

WHEN 'COPING' PAYS A CALL

The interesting thing about Mary's reply is that perhaps 'coping' creeps up on us without us realizing it. This is heartening since it would seem to indicate an element of inevitability rather than constant struggle. It's a marvellous thought that, to a certain extent, we can sit back and relax with our grief because 'coping' will turn up in its own good time. Perhaps we need to keep a look-out for 'coping' so we will recognize it when it comes round the corner. Think how many people there must be who have 'coped' and perhaps aren't even aware of it!

Perhaps it is important to remind ourselves that, for some of us at least, 'recovery' may mean we carry a proportion of our 'hurting baggage' for the rest of our lives. It is possible that we won't 'get over' great loss, in the sense that we banish all regrets, sadness and 'troughs' for ever. Maybe identifying this fact and accepting it will make this baggage a lighter load to carry. Those who have lost a loved one will still experience periods of deep sadness, and perhaps depression, especially at times of particular importance such as birthdays, wedding anniversaries and Christmas. Holidays also pose their own problems, both who to go with and where to go. We may look back on a loss and deeply regret that we didn't do things differently. We will feel sad at the thought that certain things will never be repeated; that they belong, irretrievably, to the past.

We don't 'get over' loss in the sense that, at some stage, everything gets back to normal. Loss means that life is, to some degree, never the same again. It was Sean who pointed out: 'What has happened in my life has changed me. I know I'm different – and a jolly good thing too.'

In her book about widowhood, entitled *Alone*, Katie Wiebe suggests that a widow develop a new image for herself as a single person, even though she may well still consider herself to be a married one. This idea could be applied to other losses. There's a lot to be said for perceiving and presenting yourself in a new, readjusted way:

- As close-knit, good-humoured partners who run a business, rather than as 'a childless couple'.
- As a freelance painter and decorator, rather than a man 'who once owned his own company and employed thirty people'.
- As someone with a wicked sense of humour and a big interest in opera, rather than someone 'who was once very active before becoming confined to a wheelchair'.

One of the most significant things I have ever heard, and one that has influenced me greatly, was said by the actor Anthony Hopkins when being interviewed on a radio programme. He told about the way he had struggled and wrestled with certain anxieties and problems in his life, and the fact that these had resulted in heavy drinking. One day he came to the decision that he was tired of carrying the burden of the person he was. He thought to himself, 'Well, I am an actor – so I will act as a different person.' And he did. Some might say he was simply leaving his 'baggage' of struggles and problems unresolved, that he was simply pushing them below the surface. Well, so what if he did? It worked for him. This is neither pretending nor denying; it is about using talents for acting. We all do it – though maybe not professionally. It is a conscious decision to get our resources working for us.

DECISIONS AND RENEWAL

Today, RAY is: 'a happily married man, with a broad range of interests, who has a fascinating job and is always ready to take on new opportunities'. Ten years ago Ray was: 'The man who is divorced from his wife and is struggling to keep contact with his children while juggling with badly paid self-employment'. Here's how Ray coped by making a conscious decision about his future:

> The biggest loss was, of course, losing my son and daughter. To be honest, the loss of a relationship with my former wife was a great relief – so not all loss is bad. But after the break-up, when the children moved 200 miles away, I had to accept that being a father was going to be totally different to what I had expected and hoped for.

So, Ray adjusted to being a 'distant' father. 'For the first three months after they moved I drove the 200 miles each way, every other weekend, to visit them.' This meant weekends spent largely out of doors, in all weathers, and in cafés or cinemas, because Ray and his ex-wife's relationship was so bad it was impossible to spend time with the children in their home. This was extremely unsettling for very young children, as well as unhelpful for creating an environment needed if they were to establish a new type of relationship. It also meant that Ray had to find somewhere to stay and extra expense in keeping the children warm, fed and entertained.

> I was self-employed and, what with maintenance payments and my own living expenses plus the cost of the petrol, it was hard to avoid working weekends, too. So, I sat down and tried to put my feelings and emotions to one side and think rationally. I resolved that I had to make a life for myself, and I also realized that I would be no good to the children if I wasn't emotionally independent.
>
> My wife and I had parted very acrimoniously. She had said to me: 'The children won't need you. Someone else will be the male replacement in their lives.' So the decision to further reduce what little contact I had was all the harder. But, still trying to think rationally, and with a pretty good idea of the kind of damage that feuding parents must inflict

on children, I decided that their attachment to their mother was vital and I mustn't muck that up. In addition to this, I felt I had to make a life for myself in the place where I lived and where I had an income. Intellectually, I felt I had made the right decision. Emotionally, I felt terribly guilty. I was very sad and I was very angry, but I just had to make this decision.

Afterwards Ray settled for seeing his children when they stayed with him in the school holidays and he telephoned them regularly in between. He says:

Certainly I would have liked more contact, other than simply paying maintenance – to be involved in their schooling, their problems, their general upbringing – but my ex-wife didn't want that and I didn't want to fight her through the courts. The decision to stop driving to see them every two weeks was a battle between my mind and my feelings, and it was one I knew my brain had to win – for the children's sakes, as well as for my own eventual peace of mind and my future life.

After Ray had made his decision he battled and wrestled with it for a further three months. It was another man who helped him through this period. Doug was Ray's boss and together the two men ran a small building business in the West Midlands. Ray says:

Basically, Doug let me talk. As we built, painted and decorated people's houses, I talked and talked about how I felt about the children, the awful feelings I had towards my ex-wife, how much I hated my former father-in-law. I talked non-stop for three months.

I found Doug so helpful and I shall be grateful to him for the rest of my life. And yet he said nothing. He offered no advice, no comparable experiences, no 'pearls of wisdom' – maybe he wasn't listening half the time. But he was a life-saver. Doug was like a dustbin for all the junk in my head and he seemed prepared to be that. Just being able to talk saved me.

Ray made it his business to cope. He made a hard but definite decision about the future, affecting both himself and that of his children. MARIE also constructed a 'survival system' for herself after losing both her husband and any chance of having a child. Today Marie is a confident person who holds a management job where she is responsible for several hundred people.

Twenty-five years ago she was married to a health care professional and, since Marie couldn't have children, the couple were on the brink of adopting a baby. The child's room was ready; all the plans were made. And then Marie's husband left her. Out of the blue he told her he was having an affair, that the woman was pregnant, and they had decided to set up home together. Marie had not suspected a thing.

Soon after her loss, Marie spent several weeks in America with her sister. On her return she found that her husband had not only removed all her furnishings but her personal belongings too, and these were being used by his girlfriend. 'With hindsight, I acted on bad advice from friends and my sister to visit America,' Marie says. She describes the next year as 'a complete nightmare'. Her father died, and also her dog and cat. 'I honestly thought I would never smile again.'

Her doctor prescribed tranquillizers and sleeping pills. Within days she had thrown away the tranquillizers and kept the sleeping pills to use once a week, 'So that I got one good night's sleep.' From that early stage Marie was showing a degree of control over her circumstances. She made the decision to accept the fact her marriage had ended and to create a new life – although she realized that, as a divorced person, she would never be able to adopt. She decided it was important to care for her health, to eat regularly and properly – and when she ate, to lay the table and dress nicely. 'I didn't want my standards to drop; I wanted to keep my self-respect.' Marie tried to find positive factors in all that had happened and discovered it was pleasant to be able to watch all the television programmes she enjoyed, that she no longer had to wash and starch the white coats her husband had worn for his work. She decided not to grieve publicly, 'I didn't want to burden my friends', so she cried in private. Instead, she decided never to refuse offers of help, gladly accepted invitations out to the theatre and to dinner, to share holidays and take up tennis once more.

Marie says she spent that first year in shock, the next five with the shadow of the loss over her life. At the end of that first year she began to notice subtle changes – she was laughing at television programmes, and she was thinking about new opportunities. She landed a job which she found enormously stimulating.

Now, twenty-five years later, and with a partner of long standing, Marie feels she has never really 'recovered'. Low points have been when her ex-husband's baby arrived and when her sister's baby was born. But she transferred her feelings to building relationships with friends' and her sister's children, and keeps in close touch to this day. Now that this generation is beginning to have children Marie is, once again, feeling the hurt of her own childlessness.

Rather than 'get over it' Marie has learned to live with her loss. From time to time she and her partner even see her ex-husband, who was eventually divorced from his second wife. Oddly enough, she still dreams about him returning to her, although she wouldn't want him now. Marie says that the secret of success for 'life after loss' is in accepting change. She sees the major factors involved are in accepting that:

- Loss has lifelong implications.
- There is no escaping the changes in your personality.
- No relationship will ever be the same because you are not the same.
- There is no eradicating completely the feelings of pain.
- There must be no bitterness, which is self-destructive.

LEARNING TO LIVE WITH LOSS

For Sean, Mary, Ray and Marie – and all of us who are like them – there is no doubting the struggles, the heartache and the inside pain that they have experienced and on occasions still do have. Each one of them is a survivor but each of them has surprised themselves. They would not pretend to be terribly special and are no different to you or me. What they have discovered is that grieving is a normal and necessary response to loss. They have learned from very hard experiences that there are no short-cuts or ways of avoiding the awful hurt caused by loss.

What has, however, become increasingly clear is that we do not have to remain as victims of what life, past or present, hurls at us. There is that in-built desire to survive, as well as a formidable natural healing potential within all of us. Both may need to be 'kick-started' to get us moving. That is almost the most difficult and dangerous period of loss, the time when apathy, lethargy and depression invade our senses. But depression is not a terminal state: it can be beaten.

It is not at all surprising that, faced with the uphill struggles that loss presents us with, we feel afraid. We are only human after all. But the question is: Do we need to remain afraid? That is a different matter altogether.

Bad things happen to all people. Loss is as much a part of life as happiness, success, achievement, fulfilment. When we experience loss, it becomes part of our history – the baggage of experiences we shall always carry with us. Our reactions to our losses contribute to making us the kind of people we are today – for better or for worse. 'Getting over it' may mean, then, not forgetting the past altogether, not wiping out bad experiences or moving to a stage where it's as though they never happened. Instead, it is a matter of learning to accommodate past grief, of exercising a degree of control over the hurting times, of turning life around so we move forward carrying a manageable knapsack of 'emotional baggage' on our back – rather than being bowed down with the burden of trying to drag along a huge trunk.

One thing more needs to be said. We have already made it absolutely clear that there are no 'blueprints'. Not one of the people who have shared their lives with us is the 'perfect' model. Like you, they have had to struggle with the fact of their loss, with themselves and with the particular circumstances confronting them. Each one of us is as different as the loss we face. How and how long we grieve, and how we go on to cope will be quite individual. It will be our own special and absolutely unique 'personal' story'.

Useful Addresses

The following organizations represent just a few of the very many self-help and voluntary groups around the country. New ones are starting up all the time. Some are national and others operate on a local basis. For fuller information as to what may be available to help your particular loss, consult the reference department of your local library or your Citizens' Advice Bureau. The organizations included here are listed alphabetically under each subject category. For those who write, charities and voluntary organizations all appreciate a stamped addressed envelope.

Death Loss
CRUSE (counselling, advice and information on bereavement)
Cruse House, 126 Sheen Road, Richmond, Surrey TW9 1UR. Telephone 081 332 7227 (helpline).

Jewish Bereavement Counselling Service (bereavement counselling and support for members of the Jewish community; at present operating in North and South-West London and the London borough of Redbridge)
c/o Visitation Committee, Woburn House, Tavistock Square,

London WC1H 0EZ. Telephone 071 387 4300 ext. 227 (office hours); 081 349 0839 (answerphone).

Lesbian and Gay Bereavement Project
Vaughn M. Williams Centre, Colindale Hospital, London NW9 5HG. Telephone 081 455 8894 (helpline).

National Association of Widows/Widows Advisory Trust
54–57 Allison Street, Digbeth, Birmingham B5 5TH. Telephone 021 643 8348.

War Widows Association of Great Britain
52 West Street, Gorseinon, Swansea SA4 4AF. Telephone 0792 896219.

Death Loss (Children)
The Compassionate Friends (befriending organization for parents of children – any age, including adult – who have died from any cause)
53 North Street, Bristol BS3 1EN. Telephone 0272 539 639 (helpline).

The Foundation for the Study of Infant Deaths (cot death research and support)
35 Belgrave Square, London SW1X 8QB. Telephone 071 235 1721 (24-hour helpline).

ISSUE, The National Fertility Association,
509 Aldridge Road, Great Barr, Birmingham B44 8NA. Telephone 021 344 4414.

The Miscarriage Association
c/o Clayton Hospital, Northgate, Wakefield, West Yorkshire WF1 3JS. Telephone 0924 200799.

Parents of Murdered Children Support Group (bereaved parents as a result of murder or manslaughter)
c/o Ms Pennicard, 92 Corbets Tey Road, Upminster, Essex RM14 2BA. Telephone 0708 640400.

SANDS, Stillbirth and Neonatal Death Society (support for bereaved parents)
28 Portland Place, London W1N 4DE. Telephone 071 436 5881 (helpline).

Health
Breast Care and Mastectomy Association of Great Britain (information and support)
15–19 Britten Street, London SW3 3TZ. Telephone 071 867 1103 (helpline).

Limbless Association
31 The Mall, Ealing, London W5 2PX. Telephone 081 579 1758.

LINK, British Centre for Deafened People (people deafened in adult life)
19 Hartfield Road, Eastbourne, East Sussex BN21 2AR. Voice/Minicom 0323 638230.

Macmillan Cancer Fund (skilled care and support for people with cancer and their families; Macmillan nurses)
Anchor House, 15–19 Britten Street, London SW3 3TZ. Telephone 071 351 7811.

Rainbow Centre for Children with Cancer and Life-Threatening Illness (support for children and families)
PO Box 604, Bristol BS99 1SW. Telephone 0272 736228.

Job Loss/Retirement
Fairbridge (to motivate young unemployed)
5 Westminster Bridge Road, London SE1 7XW. Telephone 071 928 1704.

Instant Muscle Ltd (counselling and training for unemployed and disadvantaged)
84 North End Road, London W14 9ES. Telephone 071 603 2604.

Project Fullemploy (inner-city community development, working

115

with black and minority groups; includes organizational training; provides customized training packages and equal opportunities programmes to private sector)
91 Brick Lane, London E1 6QN. Telephone 071 377 9536.

Marriage/Relationships
Both Parents Forever (rights for grandparents, parents and children; helps trace and return children in child abduction cases)
39 Cloonmore Avenue, Orpington, Kent BR6 9LE. Telephone 0689 854343.

Catholic Marriage Advisory Council
Clitherow House, 1 Blythe Mews, Blythe Road, London W14 0NW. Telephone 071 371 1341.

Children Need Grandparents (advice for grandparents refused access)
2 Surrey Way, Laindon West, Basildon, Essex SS15 6PS. Telephone 0268 414607.

Divorce Conciliation and Advisory Service (for parents to maintain workable arrangements for joint care of children)
38 Ebury Street, London SW1W 0LU. Telephone 071 730 2422.

Families Need Fathers (help with problems of maintaining a child's relationship with both parents following separation or divorce)
134 Curtain Road, London EC2A 3AR. Telephone 081 886 0970.

Gingerbread (support for one-parent families)
35 Wellington Street, London WC2E 7BN. Telephone 071 240 0953.

Jewish Marriage Council
23 Ravenshurst Avenue, London NW4 4EE. Telephone 081 203 6211 (24-hour crisis line).

MATCH, Mothers Apart from their Children, c/o B.M. Problems, London WC1N 3XX.

National Council for the Divorced and Separated
13 High Street, Little Shelford, Cambridge CB2 5ES. Telephone 0533 700595.

National Council for One-Parent Families
255 Kentish Town Road, London NW5 2LX. Telephone 071 267 1361; Fax 071 482 4851.

Relate, National Marriage Guidance
Herbert Gray College, Little Church Street, Rugby, Warwickshire CV21 3AP. Telephone 0788 573241.

Pets

Death of an Animal Friend is a booklet which deals with bereavement for pet owners. It costs £2.50 from The Society for Companion Animal Studies, 1A Hilton Road, Milngavie, Glasgow G62 7DN. Telephone 041 956 5950.

Good Grief is a free leaflet exploring pet loss and is available from the charity PRO Dogs, Rocky Bank, 4–6 New Road, Ditton, Aylesford, Maidstone, Kent ME20 6AD. Telephone 0732 848499. Also offers advice on protecting dogs in a will.

Other

Age-Link (Sunday afternoon monthly outings and provision of tea to housebound lonely elderly)
Suite 9, The Manor House, The Green, Southall, Middlesex UB2 4BJ. Telephone 081 571 5234.

Christian Council on Ageing (exploring Christian potential of old age)
c/o Epworth House, Stuart Street, Derby DE1 2EQ.

MIND, National Association for Mental Health (for information on where to get help with emotional problems)
22 Harley Street, London W1N 2ED. Telephone 071 637 0741.

Single Concern Group (for lonely and socially isolated people)
PO Box 4, High Street, Goring-on-Thames RG8 9DN. Telephone
0491 873195.

Victims Helpline
St Leonard's, Nuttall Street, London N1 5LZ. Telephone 071 729
1252 (24-hour helpline); Minicom (for people with hearing
difficulties) 071 613 3453. (Face-to-face counselling by appointment only.)

Victim Support (information and support for victims of crime)
National Office, Cranmer House, 39 Brixton Road, London SW9
6DZ. Telephone 071 735 9166.

Further Reading

Attachment, Loss and Grief Therapy (Routledge), Nina Leick &
   Marianne Davidson-Neilson.
Bereavement (Tavistock), Colin Murray Parkes.
Causing Death and Saving Lives (Penguin), Jonathan Glover.
Comfort for Depression (Sheldon Press), Janet Horwood.
The Courage to Grieve (Cedar), Judy Tatelbaum.
On Death and Dying (Routledge), Elizabeth Kubler Ross.
The Death of a Child (Julia MacRae Books), Tessa Williams.
Dying (Penguin), John Hinton.
Final Exit (Hemlock Society), Derek Humphrey.
Good Grief (Fount), W Sydney Callaghan.
A Grief Observed (Faber), C S Lewis.
Grieving for Change (Geoffrey Chapman), Gerald A Arbuckle.
Healing into Life and Death (Gateway), Stephen Levine.
Helping Children to Cope with Grief (Sheldon Press), Rosemary
   Wells.
The Hospice Alternative: Living with Dying (Souvenir Press),
   Margaret Manning.
Illness as Metaphor (Penguin), Susan Sontag.
The Little Book of Life and Death (Arkana), D E Harding.

Living with Death and Dying (Sovereign Press), Elizabeth Kubler Ross.

Living with Grief (Sheldon Press), Dr Tony Lake.

Living Through Personal Crisis (Sheldon Press), Ann Kaiser Sterns.

Losing a Parent (Sheldon Press), Fiona Marshall.

Mud and Stars: Impact of Hospice Experience on the Church Ministry of Healing (Sobell).

A Necessary End (Papermac), Julia Neuberger and John A White.

The Oxford Book of Death (Oxford University Press), D J Enright.

When Bad Things Happen to Good People (Pan), Harrold S Kushner.